Testimonials for Paul Sullivan and ARISE Go-to-Market®

Professional and Effective Team

We hired Paul's team based on a recommendation from our ABM technology partner, and it has been one of the best experiences we've had. The whole team caught on very quickly to our business model and was able to help us effectively create customer personas, associated messaging, and create relevant content quickly. Their comfort level with our tech stack (ABM, HubSpot Marketing, Sales and CRM, and Cognism) was impressive and critical to moving quickly. I have truly come to think of them as part of my marketing team.

—**Heidi Humphries**
Sales and Marketing Director
Direct Sourcing DSSI, Inc

Marketing Strategy, Content and HubSpot Setup for Outsourced Software Development

Paul and the team are not only experts in marketing strategy, the tech sector, and HubSpot, they also take great care and ownership of the campaigns they work on. I can highly recommend them as a collaborative, honest, and results driven agency—particularly for fast growing B2B tech/SaaS businesses.

—**James Hodgson**
UK CEO, 300Brains

BIAS Helped Take Our HubSpot Instance to the Next Level!

We recommend the team at ARISE highly. After deciding that our HubSpot instance and pipeline were no longer fit for purpose, they helped us to completely revolutionize our approach. Rob took the time to listen to our specific requirements and helped create a bespoke setup that included automated repeat tasks, task workflows for our Account Execs, and reporting dashboards for easier analysis and optimization. We now have a solution that is scalable, ready for our next phase of growth, and enables our SDRs and AEs to focus on what really matters—driving and converting pipeline. If you're looking for a trusty HubSpot partner, then get in touch with Paul.

—**Jody Leon**
Chief Marketing Officer
DSMN8

A Unique Combination of Strategy, Tech Know-how and Implementation

HUBX decided to migrate from Pipedrive to HubSpot to take advantage of a fully integrated CRM and marketing automation solution that seamlessly connected customer information through to the customer success and service teams. We also use Drift playbooks extensively for visitor tracking and comms. We needed an agency that understood how to optimize multiple elements in our sales and marketing tech stack to deliver the best insights and customer experience, understand what converted and why, as well as lead the migration, making sure that all valuable data was retained.

I found Paul extremely insightful, knowledgeable, and also up for challenging many assumptions we'd made along the way. The difference with Paul at BIAS is that not only does he understand the what and why but he also knows the right way to deploy the tech to get the best result. Paul was a pleasure to work with and was doggedly determined to make sure that challenges we met along the way were solved, putting in extra hours and going the extra mile. I would highly recommend Paul and ARISE GTM to any B2B SaaS organization looking to optimize their tech approach to CRM and inbound marketing.

—**Ray De Silva,**
Chief Commercial Officer
HubX Capital

Vantage Accelerator Workshop Partner—Amazing Job!

Paul has worked with us to support 3 of our accelerator cohorts and more than 50 startups this year by delivering workshops on PLG. The content and advice given to the founders has played a vital role in refining their growth strategy pre and post-fundraising. Feedback from the founders after the workshop was amazing. Paul delivered an interactive and engaging workshop that demonstrated his extensive knowledge on all things PLG and more!

—**Sophie Scoular**
Head of Program, Vantage Accelerator

A Strong Partner in HubSpot Implementation and Growth Strategies

We recently partnered with ARISE to take our marketing efforts to the next level. Our goal was twofold: improve our search engine optimization (SEO) ranking and leverage the HubSpot platform to generate more qualified sales leads for DSSI (www.directsourcing.com). We're happy to report that ARISE exceeded our expectations. From the outset, ARISE impressed us with their in-depth knowledge of HubSpot's capabilities. However, what truly set them apart was their commitment to understanding our unique business model. They conducted a thorough competitive analysis and took the time to delve into our specific needs and goals. This resulted in a customized implementation plan that directly addressed our challenges and opportunities.

But ARISE's expertise extended beyond the software itself. Their team showcased a keen understanding of current marketing trends and how to utilize them within the HubSpot platform. They provided valuable insights into inbound marketing strategies, content creation best practices, and marketing automation techniques—all meticulously tailored to our industry and target audience.

This forward-thinking approach ensured that we not only implemented HubSpot effectively, but also optimized our overall marketing strategy for maximum impact. Throughout the entire process, BIAS maintained clear and consistent communication. They kept us informed every step of the way and readily addressed any questions or concerns. A special shout-out to Paul and Fawn, whose professionalism, courtesy, and unwavering support throughout the project were invaluable.

—**Amit Mendiratta**
Leader in Source To Pay and Supply
Chain Digital Transformation
Direct Sourcing, DSSI Inc

GO-TO-MARKET

UNCOVERED

PAUL SULLIVAN

GO-TO-MARKET

UNCOVERED

HOW TO
Successfully
Launch a Product
and Drive Sustainable,
Long-Term **Revenue Growth**

WILEY

Published by John Wiley & Sons, Inc., Hoboken, New Jersey.
Published simultaneously in Canada.

For general information on our other products and services or for technical support, please contact our Customer Care Department within the United States at (800) 762-2974, outside the United States at (317) 572-3993 or fax (317) 572-4002.

Wiley also publishes its books in a variety of electronic formats. Some content that appears in print may not be available in electronic formats. For more information about Wiley products, visit our website at www.wiley.com.

Library of Congress Cataloging-in-Publication Data is Available:

ISBN 978-1-394-32888-8 (Hardcover)
ISBN 978-1-394-32891-8 (ePDF)
ISBN 978-1-394-32890-1 (ePub)

Cover Design: Wiley
Cover Images: © Ilham/Adobe Stock, © MicroOne/Adobe Stock
Author Photo: Courtesy of PAUL SULLIVAN

SKY10098050_020725

I want to dedicate this book to my grandfather, Arthur James Henry Sullivan, who was one of my biggest admirers even when my actions weren't always admirable. Always there to listen, guide, and support me. You were a critical voice in my ever-expanding desire for growth and adventure. I miss our conversations and hope this makes you proud when you look down on me.

Gone but not forgotten, ever x.

21.02.1929–12.06.2014

Contents

Preface

Go-to-market (GTM) strategy isn't just an area of specialism for me; it's a driver of my daily routine, and those that know me for it have often referred to me as a kid in a playground when I make something happen that makes it easier for others to understand their current predicament.

In early October 2024, I had been working on a dashboard for HubSpot that my clients could use to quickly identify their correct Ideal Customer Profile (ICP) from their data, not some reverse-engineered profile from the sales team. Not that it's an impossible task, but one that not everyone using HubSpot would quickly figure out. I'd been in the office that weekend trying to figure it out because building a GTM strategy should include segmentation for companies that have been in market for some time.

Once I solved it, I immediately dropped it into my customers' portal thanks to Supered, a tool designed to help with internal product and process adoption. It also allows you to build in HubSpot, save it to the cloud, and one-click deploy it to multiple client portals afterward.

On the following Monday, I immediately ran upstairs to my client, who is based in the same building as me, grabbed Sam, their CMO, and asked for feedback on what was missing. We settled on understanding how long contacts from their best-performing ICP sat in a particular lifecycle stage in the marketing and sales funnel. This is because you can then dive into where those contacts typically engaged with the business and see how you can optimize those stages to improve velocity across the revenue lifecycle.

I now use this report and a data hygiene report to immediately assess the health of a HubSpot portal, a crucial part of my product and service offering and to help my clients immediately understand where to focus their efforts and why.

Throughout this book, we'll explore:

- The fundamental importance of GTM strategies in business success
- Common pitfalls and challenges in GTM planning and execution
- A detailed overview of the ARISE GTM Methodology® and its application
- Practical insights for startups, scaling teams, and enterprise organizations
- The integration of GTM strategies with modern tools like HubSpot

As we journey through the chapters, you'll gain a deeper understanding of how to craft a GTM strategy that launches your product successfully and ensures long-term growth and customer satisfaction. We'll explore a modern GTM playbook and discover how the ARISE GTM Methodology® can transform your market entry and expansion approach.

The ability to effectively bring products and services to market can mean the difference between success and obscurity. As a veteran of the technology industry and a witness to countless product launches, I've seen firsthand the critical role that a well-crafted go-to-market strategy plays in a company's journey.

This book—which you hold in your hands or perhaps view on your screen—is more than just a guide; it's a compass for navigating the complex terrain of modern market entry. The ARISE Go-To-Market Methodology® presented here represents a significant leap forward in how we approach GTM strategies, especially in B2B SaaS, fintech, and technology-enabled businesses.

What sets this work apart is its practical approach. While many business books offer theoretical frameworks, this one provides a concrete, actionable methodology that has been tested and refined in the real world. The ARISE framework—Assess, Research, Ideate, Strategise, and Execute—offers a comprehensive road map that can be adapted to businesses of all sizes, from nimble startups to established enterprises.

As you delve into these pages, you'll find insights that challenge conventional wisdom and strategies that push the boundaries of traditional GTM thinking. You'll find this book to be jam-packed with real-world examples, clear and detailed explanations, and practical tips.

Whether you're a seasoned marketing executive looking to refine your approach, a startup founder preparing for your first product launch, or a business student eager to understand the intricacies of bringing innovations to market, this book has something valuable to offer you.

We live in a world where the pace of change is relentless and the margin for error is slim, so having a robust GTM strategy is not just beneficial—it's essential. This book equips you with the tools and knowledge to craft such a strategy, helping you turn your product vision into an in-market reality.

As you embark on this journey through the ARISE methodology, I encourage you to approach it with an open mind and a readiness to apply these concepts to your unique business challenges. The insights you gain here have the potential to transform not just how you approach market entry but also how you think about your entire business strategy.

May this book serve as your guide to navigating the complexities of modern markets, and may the ARISE methodology illuminate your path to success.

Introduction

As the creator of the ARISE Go-to-Market Methodology®, I've spent more than 15 years shaping GTM strategies for tech and service companies. This experience led me to develop ARISE, a comprehensive framework that combines proven optimization techniques with cutting-edge technology to drive growth for B2B SaaS, fintech, and technology-enabled businesses. Its comprehensive nature ensures that no aspect of your go-to-market strategy is overlooked, giving you a heightened sense of security about its thoroughness.

ARISE stands for Assess, Research, Ideate, Strategise, and Execute. Each stage is designed to be thorough yet agile, empowering companies to rapidly increase their ROI on technology investments and strategic initiatives. What sets ARISE apart is its practicality. It doesn't require a large team or extended timelines. In fact, we can often implement the full methodology in just 30 days for early-stage startups, giving you the power to make significant changes in a short time.

One of the key strengths of ARISE is its proactive approach to experimentation and adaptation. We anticipate potential market forces and performance challenges, building contingency plans directly into our recommended tactics. This level of foresight and flexibility is rare in the consultancy world.

While ARISE was initially built for product companies, we've successfully applied it to service providers as well. The practical and scalable methodology works equally well for startups, scale-ups, and enterprise teams. It provides a clearly defined, best-practice model that allows us to operate at the right speed, depth, and scale for each unique situation, giving you the reassurance that it can be tailored to your specific needs.

In this book, I'll guide you through each stage of the ARISE methodology, sharing insights and practical strategies you can apply to your go-to-market efforts. Whether you're launching a new product, entering a new market, or looking to optimize your current GTM approach, the principles of ARISE can help you achieve sustainable growth and competitive advantage.

The primary goal of your go-to-market strategy is to enhance customer experience by offering superior products and/or competitive pricing and creating a clear plan to penetrate a defined market or target audience. Your initial focus should involve defining the target market, determining if prospective customers exist within that base, and deciding on a value proposition.

This is where the ARISE GTM Methodology®, Strategy, or Framework comes into play. It's a playbook that delivers a revenue operations outcome, designed on strong product marketing principles and optimization frameworks, coupled with buyer enablement and customer onboarding. However, it wasn't designed with revenue operations in mind.

In truth, I think most GTM sucks because there's no widely accepted definitive explanation of what it means; for example, salespeople will call selling go-to-market, and marketers will consider marketing part of the go-to-market motion. Yet product marketing is a different skill set to today's marketers; they are multi-disciplinarians who unite the product with the rest of the organization. On this basis, I decided that the current understanding of GTM was broken and ARISE was born.

Why Now

Between 2010 and 2022, the VC and PE taps were wide open, and cloud-based technology firms were raising round after round after round. Then came COVID, and the money fizzled out. I was already ahead of the curve, calling out poor fiscal management when your strategy was "I'll raise (bail myself out) when I had burned too much cash," but hey, it seems when the money's in, the wits are out.

I have been calling out the ABM, ABX, and AB Everything Acronym merchants as "just good marketing," publicly saying on LinkedIn that they should accept account-based marketing or a target account strategy as the proper way to do business.

It's widely acknowledged that I have been asking why, if your GTM planning was so accurate, you couldn't name the few hundred or thousand good-fit prospects or target accounts in any geographical location your product was fit for. If you could, the tools are there to only target and focus on them, which would reduce wastage in marketing spend, increase brand awareness within the niche or market segment, and improve win rates, customer acquisition costs (CAC), and payback. Win-win.

We've been calling for better alignment between marketing and sales for as long as I can remember, and the same with personalization at scale, again forever. But in the search for evermore differentiation and category creation, people added more acronyms, bringing more complexity to something that should simply be part of solid business governance. Believe me, there's nothing hard with alignment except ego, lack of discipline, or a poor company culture.

Did I say Revenue Operations?

As the owner of a strategic B2B go-to-market consultancy, I find it quite rewarding to see the rise of Revenue Operations, but come on, should it really be such a big deal? No slight meant to revops people, but tech, process, and alignment should be business 101. It should be the norm, not the exception and as I said previously, something straight out of the gates, not a maturity model.

You have to do things properly for anything to work well. Anything less isn't best practice, and that's when you open yourself up to leaky funnels, shitty customers that churn and hurt your internal culture, the payback on your cost of acquisition goes through the roof, and the business starts creaking under the realization that status quo just isn't good enough.

But I digress. There will be plenty of time to discuss these models later in the book, and I was just telling you that I was ahead of the curve.

I formally designed the ARISE GTM Methodology® in 2019 during COVID-19. The driver was the constant expansion and contraction of my agency, ARISE GTM®, and the fact that whenever I scaled the business, it often coincided with an increase in churn, and I hated that. It got me thinking about how I manage and retain long 3, 4, or 5-year relationships with myself and the freelancers and offshore teams, and yet every time I try to build my local or in-house team, we'd see clients churn out in six months, and I'm too competitive and care too much about my client's experience and my business reputation to allow that to happen.

So when COVID came along, I had to decide what type of business I wanted, look at the staff, and decide if they could get me there, and they couldn't, so no furlough, I went back to scratch. I kept four clients, took a bounce-back loan, and decided to rebuild from the ground up. During COVID, I took everything out of my head, put it down on paper, and took 14 certifications: MEDDIC, MEDDPICC, Product Marketing Leadership, a raft of HubSpot Certifications, Positioning Masters, Storytelling Masters, and more. I was all in, and I wasn't going to fail again (but I did, and that story comes later).

That was the first time I had put the process into a playbook. It was nothing fancy, and if I'm honest, I still have version one sitting in a project template in my Basecamp 2 project management tool. I know, how old, but I'm now tooled out. We have ClickUp, which I still don't know how to use, and I'm looking at PSOhub because it's been designed and built to work with HubSpot, our core Customer Relationship Management (CRM) and Customer Platform. Tools form a key part of this book, and HubSpot sits at the center of the ARISE GTM Framework®. As a HubSpot consultancy partner, I designed it to be delivered and executed on the platform.

I

Introduction to Go-to-Market Strategy

"70% of GTM strategies fail as a result of misalignment between teams."

—Gartner

1

The Importance of a Robust Go-to-Market Strategy

What Is a Go-to-Market Strategy?

Before starting this first chapter, I want to define what a go-to-market (GTM) strategy is so that readers of this book understand my perspective. I see GTM as a holistic thing, not the domain of one single team or department but that of the whole, the entire organization. It's reflected in the business culture and philosophy, processes, technology, leadership, grassroots teams, finance, operations, and social policies. Ultimately, I think your customer experiences, or views, your go-to-market as your brand.

According to Gartner, an American technological research and consulting firm, "A GTM strategy is a plan that details how an organization can engage with customers to convince them to buy its product or service and gain a competitive advantage. A GTM strategy includes tactics related to pricing, sales and channels, the buying journey, new product or service launches, product rebranding, or product introduction to a new market."

In short, it's a strategic plan for launching a product or service. Let's unpack that for a minute. The easiest way I can explain go-to-market strategy is that it is how a company executes its business

3

strategy over a given period. This period is typically 12 months, although you can have a 2, 5, or 10-year strategy. For the most part, anything longer than two years is more of a plan or a hypothetical guess, as you simply cannot forecast or predict market forces (Figure 1.1).

This diagram lays it out as clearly as I can envision it. The business strategy sits at the top of the chart. Your operations, finance, and product teams are on the next layer, and then your customer-facing teams and product user data sit on the lower level.

For Startups

For early-stage startups, potentially pre- or just post-product-market fit (PMF), I expect to see the business strategy, product team, sales team, and at least a single marketing resource. However, I am a massive fan of selling your product or service first and marketing it second, as it's more straightforward to pay for marketing from a revenue-generating position than to burn through your runway marketing something to an audience you might not yet fully understand (or an audience that might not understand you).

In my experience, many startups do not have a proper finance function. Early-stage founders typically adopt a founder-led sales approach with maybe a few sales or business development reps (BDRs) until they are comfortable they have fit and forego everything else.

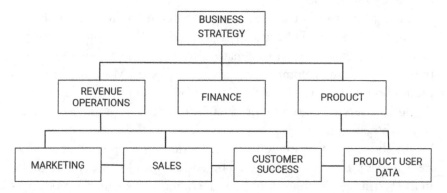

Figure 1.1 Company structure for executing the business plan.

A strong GTM play often feels like a maturity model in the business's developmental process for early-stage founders, as is a RevOps model, when, in fact, building with the end in mind is the ideal approach. There are many tools out there that can help you do this. With my expertise in HubSpot and our HubSpot CRM-enhancing GTM engine, we can remove the barriers to best practices and see more growth, data-driven decision-making, and tactical analysis with the AI.

Any founder launching a business, and it doesn't matter if it's a tech platform or a service business, should follow the three best practice principles and answer them clearly:

1. How do I convey the value of my product or service to my end user or customer?
2. How do I enable my buyer to buy from me?
3. How do I plan to onboard, retain, and expand my buyer?

This oversimplifies the GTM process, which must be redundant to digest this concept. I want to forego buzzwords and industry jargon where possible and lay out clear, easy-to-follow pathways and guidelines as we examine each stage in-depth to get your GTM firing on all cylinders.

1. How do I convey the value of my product or service to my end user or customer?
    (a) Value proposition
    (b) Positioning
    (c) Messaging
    (d) Storytelling
    (e) Customer feedback
    (f) Win/loss research
    (g) Competitive analysis
    (h) SWOT
    (i) Porters Five Forces
    (j) Jobs-to-be-done
    (k) Buyer/user persona research and interviews

2. How do I enable my buyer to buy from me?
   (a) Jobs-to-be-done
   (b) Buyer/user persona research and interviews
   (c) Win/loss interviews
   (d) Competitive analysis
   (e) Sales enablement (training, assets, technology)
   (f) Pricing strategy
   (g) Buyer funnel stages and tactics
   (h) Marketing tactics (content, events, ads, social media)
3. How do I plan to onboard, retain, and expand my buyer?
   (a) Customer onboarding framework
   (b) Customer journey map
   (c) Automated email sequences
   (d) Customer portals
   (e) Renewals playbooks
   (f) Usage-based upsell/cross-sell
   (g) What new features to ship or services to develop?
   (h) How do I measure it all?

As you can see, the exercises you perform often impact more than one stage of the GTM strategy cycle. Therefore, they must be implemented and executed repeatedly to ensure your GTM continues to align with your buyer and user audience.

In this book, we will discover the ARISE methodology, my trademark approach to GTM strategy. While it's primarily focused on B2B product companies, we have successfully used it on service companies, too. One example is a small two-person company, The Reinhart Group, run by a couple, Christina de Bueklaar and Emmanuel Stiels, where we used it to rebrand and productize their services for a Health and Wellbeing business and private health practice. I dive into this in more detail in the case studies section of the book.

For Scaling Teams

Post PMF, I expect the company to have a proper finance function, either full-time or fractional. The product team should be sharing user data into your CRM, and from my HubSpot expertise, you can connect your product to HubSpot through APIs or, as I prefer, use Mixpanel and HubSpot as a combination.

This is especially useful for product-led (PLG) companies, where user segmentation and CRM segmentation are crucial to understanding user segment drivers and translating that into marketing and sales tactics. This is a slimline tech stack, as you should use the HubSpot Customer Platform, including marketing and content hubs, sales hubs, and service hubs, simply because the single-code platform makes it easy to scale. Their embedded app cards further simpify life by dropping other third-party apps directly into your user interface, giving the ability to experience your third-party apps directly inside HubSpot, which changes the game.

Where HubSpot drops off in reporting, use Databox. Pete Caputa, the CEO, is an ex-HubSpot employee, so he knows how and why the two tools connect to enhance financial reporting right out of the CRM while keeping HubSpot at the heart of the business. It also focuses deeply on other areas of reporting so everyone across the organization benefits from the product.

Later in this book, I'll share how you bring product teams into HubSpot so that a business's revenue focus becomes a shared experience. You can make smarter decisions by reporting how feature releases impact usage through user data and correlating that with sales and marketing data. This also helps identify where significant financial impact or lack thereof comes from with feature releases. But this is how I see the world; you can disagree.

For the Enterprise

My experience with enterprise companies is in two places: strategic account-based marketing (ABM) and when they spin out a new product including moving from sales-led to product-led as a business model. The use case for the ARISE Go-To-Market Methodology® has been proven in both situations.

When the largest companies use ABM, it is almost always to outcompete their rivals in landing key accounts, so the heavy research-based element of ARISE plays a significant role in enabling this as it focuses on deep understanding of target accounts and competitive landscape.

When enterprise teams spin out a new product, you might think this should be easy due to their current size and longevity in the tech space. However, often, you hire people with different skills for enterprise business management than you would for a startup, so the skill set is ill-fitted. This is where ARISE comes into its own, and to be clear, my simplified diagram wouldn't fit most enterprise companies as they have large product marketing teams, enablement teams, multi-regional sales teams, and more, but the premise remains the same without the nuance and granularity of team specialisms.

As we traverse the book, I'll discuss innovation and account-based marketing and how the two complement each other.

Why GTM Strategies Are Crucial for Business Success

As a product and business owner, I can't stress enough how crucial it is to have a robust go-to-market strategy. I've seen firsthand how it ensures a successful product launch by providing a clear road map and helping to avoid common pitfalls. It's amazing how a well-crafted GTM strategy can streamline your processes, reducing time to market and giving you a competitive edge. However, it's just as amazing to see how many people shortcut and discount a thorough GTM approach. The number of times I've been told by prospects that they don't want to spend months on research, they want to get going, like there's some magic bullet we consultants and agencies have that immediately solves their leaky or underperforming funnel. Get real; months, maybe not, but none at all, that's sheer stupidity.

I've learned that it's not just about getting the product out there quickly; it's about doing it smartly to minimize financial risks and delay achieving PMF. You can address potential challenges proactively and use your marketing budgets more effectively by identifying those challenges early. And to do that, you have to keep speaking to people, and that starts at day one.

One of the main aspects I love most about a solid GTM strategy is how it enhances the customer experience. When we truly understand our target audience and their needs, we can tailor our product, marketing, and sales efforts to meet those needs, building customer loyalty and driving repeat business. I've seen how this approach significantly improves your customer acquisition effectiveness, helping identify the most impactful channels and messages to reach your audience. By understanding this, it makes the creative process far easier as you know the best mediums, assets, and channels to engage with.

From experience, a comprehensive GTM strategy is invaluable for market penetration and growth. It gives you a clear plan for entering or expanding within existing markets, outlining the steps you need to take to gain market share and achieve sustainable growth. It's incredibly effective in aligning your organizational efforts, ensuring that all departments, from product development to customer support, work toward the same goals.

Perhaps most importantly, I've witnessed how a robust GTM strategy can provide a real competitive advantage. By thoroughly analyzing the competitive landscape and positioning your product effectively, you can differentiate yourself and attract customers in even the most crowded markets. It helps you raise awareness about your product among your target audience, generating interest and demand, which is crucial for success.

Ultimately, I've come to understand that a GTM strategy isn't just about the initial launch; it's about ensuring long-term success. By continuously monitoring market trends, customer feedback, and competitive actions, we can make informed decisions and adapt our strategies as needed. In my role, I've repeatedly seen how a well-executed GTM strategy is essential for minimizing risks, enhancing customer experience, and achieving sustainable growth. This book's road map guides you toward your goals and contributes significantly to your overall business success.

Common Pitfalls in Your GTM Strategy

During my career, I've encountered numerous pitfalls and challenges in developing go-to-market (GTM) strategies. One of the most common issues is failing to define a clear target market, which leads to ineffective marketing efforts and wasted resources. The ARISE GTM framework has been instrumental in addressing this. During the Research stage, we conduct thorough market analyses and gather customer insights, which helps us clearly define the target market and understand customer needs.

Another challenge I've faced is insufficient market research, which can result in misaligned product offerings and ineffective strategies. The ARISE framework emphasizes comprehensive market analysis in the Research stage, including competitive intelligence and market trends, ensuring our strategies are evidence based. Over-reliance on a single marketing channel is another pitfall; ARISE's Ideate and Strategise stages encourage us to explore multiple channels and develop a multi-faceted approach to reach our audience effectively. This isn't about random experimentation, it's driven by your customer research and understanding their habits and favorite channels for collecting information about products and services like yours.

I've also seen how a lack of data-driven decision-making can lead to ineffective strategies and missed opportunities. ARISE ensures data collection and analysis, particularly in the Research and Assess stages, so solid data backs all our decisions. Ensuring product-market fit is crucial, and the Assess and Research stages focus on understanding market needs and validating this fit before moving forward.

Poor alignment across teams can lead to inconsistent messaging and ineffective execution. The ARISE framework promotes a holistic approach, ensuring all teams are aligned from research to execution. The fact that we've been calling for closer alignment of marketing and sales since the turn of the century beguiles me, allowing a whole industry to moan about best practice and then do little in the way of actually making that happen. Maybe the end of the latest bubble and growth at all costs mindset will see a return to proper business administration, or maybe not; maybe the people currently running businesses will delay and delay, harking back to the glory days of raising your way out of trouble rather than focusing on good business governance. But I digress.

Insufficient risk assessment is another common issue, and the Assess stage includes thorough risk analysis, helping you anticipate and plan for potential challenges. By deep diving into current underperformance and identifying gaps in your data, you move toward a more streamlined approach to customer acquisition, using data-driven triggers with reporting that tells stories teams can understand and execute against.

Ineffective positioning and messaging can confuse customers and hinder product or service adoption. The Ideate and Strategise stages focus on developing clear, compelling positioning and messaging based on first-party data, market insights, and competitive analysis. Additionally, inadequate sales enablement can lead to poor conversion rates. Still, the Execute stage includes comprehensive sales enablement, providing your sales teams with the right tools and knowledge they need based on the competitive and customer research previously undertaken.

Finally, neglecting customer retention often leads to high churn rates and reduced lifetime value. The ARISE framework includes customer onboarding and retention strategies, ensuring long-term success beyond the initial launch. By addressing these common pitfalls, the ARISE GTM framework provides a comprehensive approach to developing and executing effective go-to-market strategies that significantly improve your chances of success in Software-as-a-Service (SaaS), Financial Technology (Fintech), and the services industries.

What Does a Good GTM Outline Look Like?

To execute a solid GTM strategy, you must optimize eight pillars. Neglect any one of them, and you will severely decrease your ability to succeed in the long term. Nearly every founder, business leader, or GTM leader can tell you a story about how they are constantly pressured to cut a corner for speed or budget, which causes frustration and often undermines their ability to deliver results in a realistic and timely manner. Shortcuts are for suckers, as they almost always cost you more than you think in the end.

The new narrative in GTM, which has been incorrectly deployed and interpreted, is that done is better than perfect, and it is. Being agile in your approach to running campaigns is crucial for smaller, less established businesses; maybe not so for larger organizations with a well established brand. But, that doesn't mean spraying and praying and hoping for a miracle on the other end; it means once you have the complete information you need, enter the market fast and run as many experiments as possible to find out what works. You will succeed when you develop an experimental mindset: **segments and experiments;** memorize that. However, I am sure that the marketers reading this book immediately thought, well my boss will ask me about ROI, so experimentation isn't a high priority when numbers matter. I feel for you, I do, but remember, Rome wasn't built in a day and you have to sometimes stand your ground to get respect and gain more control of the marketing mix.

Poor go-to-market has seen too many founders and leadership teams fall victim to employing underperforming agencies that use flattering metrics and supportive reporting systems, allowing poor performance to continue. While agencies have a place in the GTM process, because they have specialist skills or simply augment smaller teams, you shouldn't hand responsibility to them for your businesses success. They are there to deliver a result, but the ownership of their performance is that of the leadership team. When you hand responsibility off, a culture of blame often develops with a revolving door of agencies and consultants with no effective change occurring, just tick-box activity. When this happens, eventually the internal culture suffers because staff start to disbelieve change will ever happen, or in severe cases, your staff are working against you to ensure failure to maintain the status quo. Additionally, some founders go through senior management like a hot knife through butter, causing chaos, misalignment, and a further deteriorating employment culture.

I'm talking about people here because people are the key asset to successful GTM; technology is just an enablement tool. Wrong leaders, you fail; wrong team, you fail. Ultimately, it's about the right bums in the right seats. Achieve that, and you will likely see a more considerable improvement in results than any one SaaS platform brings.

But is this all it takes, or is there more to it? Are there fundamentals we need to adopt, such as best practices, frameworks, methodologies, flywheels, and funnels, just to name a few? Potentially, yes, and there are some I'd like to dive into. As I mentioned earlier, I believe there are eight fundamental pillars you have to master in order to build a robust go-to-market strategy—one that is customer-centric, sustainable, and profitable and we'll cover those in the next chapter.

2

The Eight Pillars of GTM Strategy

I'D LIKE TO kick things off with this: "Without structure there is no success."

In fact, I'd go as far as to say that even creativity comes from structure. Hear me out. Even the most creative of artists say they have a process, so there's no way unstructured approaches to anything bode well. At best, it's haphazard and unmeasurable, and that just leads to further frustration. And I can't even count the number of times I've asked founders or early-stage teams, "How did you achieve that?" and they can't explain it. They weren't tracking the right things, so their data and reporting were also useless.

Why am I kicking off so contentiously? Because I want to emphasize that you need to believe in an order rather than participate in one. That's why I want you to gather around the eight pillars of go-to-market strategy and ensure you enshrine them in your forward thinking and strategic planning.

In the last chapter, I explained that any founder launching a business, and it doesn't matter if it's a tech platform or a service business, should follow the three best practice principles:

1. How do I convey the value of my product or service to my end user or customer?
2. How do I enable my buyer to buy from me?
3. How do I plan to onboard, retain, and expand my buyer?

Let me now explain why.

Pillar #1: Discovery

Discovery is the bedrock of your strategic efforts. I'm a massive fan of evidence-backed strategic decisions, whether from first-party or third-party data and preferably a combination of the two. There is no reverse engineering to desired outcomes or having decisions solely made on gut feel; however, I recognize this is important for experienced GTM professionals, less so for newbies and inexperienced teams.

For this part of the strategic process, you will cover areas such as the business case, the size of the available market, competitive SWOT analysis, Porter's Five Forces, win/loss interviews where possible, customer feedback, and a competitive intelligence review of your direct and indirect competition.

The purpose of these activities is to use this research as a baseline for your forward thinking, ideation, and strategic decision-making during the execution of ARISE. The outcomes will ultimately help develop competitive strategies for mature companies, battle cards and sales sequences for your sales teams, and content strategies for marketing, enabling you to understand and defend your market position at all times.

This might be a good time to let you know that, at the time of this writing, we are building ARISE as an app called Leevr for HubSpot users so that you can run your strategy directly from the CRM. That's why I implore you to choose HubSpot over Salesforce, and I'll dive into that later.

Pillar #2: Personas, Segmentation, and Jobs to Be Done

Conduct customer and user research interviews to understand who is buying what and why and who is using what and how. I'm a huge fan of persona (user and customer) interviews for context and clarity of the job at hand, as well as running jobs-to-be-done interviews, and workshops to completely understand what each segment uses your product or service to achieve. Then, correlate the data between the two in your messaging and storytelling for the identified customer segments. This will drive your marketing and sales messaging and website copy forward and should immediately give you improved results. Prepare A/B tests of your messaging and try logical and emotive messaging to see what works best, mixing problem and outcome statements to see what drives results for your organization.

Next, formulate your hypothesis based on your customer segments. You need to hypothesize what revenue streams will come from which segments of your customers to prepare to plan your customer acquisition program strategically. This can also help you understand which segment to target first and how much of a budget to apply to each segment. Build financial prediction models based on historical performance and use this to drive budget decisions for your new financial goals. Use the jobs-to-be-done framework to establish the job your persona is trying to perform by hiring your product or service and understand how they decided on a product or service provider that includes a business like yours.

Pillar #3: Positioning, Messaging, and Value Proposition

After you complete your customer and competitive research, you will define your value proposition, messaging, positioning statements, and storytelling frameworks for each segment, product, or service. You should start this at the same time as the persona work to test your outcomes and theories during the persona interviews. The idea is that you are looking at this whole process objectively and not to support or deny any theories you may currently have. Use open-ended questions, record the interviews with an AI tool, and ensure that all recordings sit within your CRM so that the data is accessible to the AI there, too.

Avoid vanilla positioning. Try to lean toward the outcomes your product delivers rather than the features or benefits of your product. Remember, you can position yourself to different buyers, users, and decision-makers. It's rarely a one-size-fits-all situation. This is another reason you need tools like HubSpot's smart content for the CMS or something like that, maybe Mutiny because you can serve different segments of your audience targeted messaging on your website with them. But don't let me get sidetracked with solutions just yet. Vanilla GTM programs deliver vanilla results, and if you follow my prescribed methodology, I can assure you that this will no longer be the case for you.

As I mentioned, when building your messaging, lean into outcome driven messaging and make it emotional. Use a storytelling framework like the hero's journey or something similar to help you craft a story that resonates with your buyer and can be remembered.

Popularized by Joseph Campbell, the hero's journey framework involves a protagonist who embarks on an adventure, faces challenges, and ultimately emerges transformed. To apply the hero's journey to an SaaS company's marketing strategy, you can structure your marketing narrative around the customer's journey, positioning them as the hero and your SaaS product as the guide or mentor. This method creates a strong emotional connection and illustrates the transformative impact of the product.

Here's how you can implement this approach:

1. **Ordinary World**: Introduce your target customer in their current state, facing challenges that your product or service solution can address. For example, a project manager who struggles with disorganized workflows and missed deadlines.
2. **Call to Adventure**: Present the opportunity for change, perhaps through an ad or content highlighting the potential for improvement in their work processes.
3. **Refusal of the Call**: Acknowledge customers' hesitation about adopting a new software solution. This could be concerns about implementation time, cost, or learning curve.
4. **Meeting the Mentor**: Position your product or service as the guide to help them overcome challenges. Use your marketing

materials to demonstrate how your solution provides the tools and support they need.

5. **Crossing the Threshold**: Show how customers begin their journey with your product, perhaps through a free trial or onboarding process.
6. **Tests, Allies, Enemies**: Illustrate the initial challenges of implementing the software and how your customer support and features help overcome these obstacles.
7. **Approach to the Inmost Cave**: Depict how customers start to see real benefits from using your product or service, building toward a major breakthrough.
8. **Ordeal**: Present a significant challenge your customer faces, which your product or service helps them overcome. This could be a critical project or a major business goal.
9. **Reward**: Showcase the success and benefits of using your product or service. Use specific metrics and outcomes to make this tangible.
10. **The Road Back**: Demonstrate how customers continue to use your product to maintain their success and face new challenges.
11. **Resurrection**: Highlight a final, transformative success that cements the value of your product or service in the customer's business processes.
12. **Return with the Elixir**: Show how your customers have been transformed by using your product or service, perhaps becoming more efficient, profitable, or innovative. This is where you can incorporate testimonials and case studies.

Throughout this journey, focus on:

- **Emotional Engagement**: Use storytelling to connect with potential customers emotionally by addressing their pain points and aspirations.
- **Simplifying Complex Concepts**: Use the narrative structure to break down your SaaS product's complex features into relatable, easy-to-understand benefits.
- **Visual Storytelling**: Incorporate images, videos, and infographics to make your story more engaging and memorable.

- **Consistency Across Channels**: Maintain a consistent narrative across all marketing touchpoints, from your website to email campaigns and social media.
- **User-Generated Content**: Encourage satisfied customers to share their success stories, creating authentic testimonials that fit your overarching narrative.

So, as you can see, by applying the hero's journey framework, you can create a compelling marketing narrative that resonates with potential customers, showcases the value of your product or service, and guides prospects through their decision-making process.

This approach helps potential customers see themselves as the hero of their own story, with your SaaS or fintech product playing the crucial role of the mentor or guide that enables their success. But if that structure is too complicated for you, there are more simple storytelling frameworks that can still provide great value. Try answering these questions and see where you end up:

1. **Target audience identification**: Define your key demographic or persona.
   For instance, Mark is a Marketing Director overseeing the creation, distribution, and analysis of the company's B2B marketing campaigns.
2. **Current situation assessment**: Describe their world without your product.
   Presently, Mark grapples with extracting meaningful insights from numerous concurrent, multi-channel marketing initiatives.
3. **The antagonist**: Identify their existing workaround. How are they attempting to solve their problem now?
   Mark tries to bridge the gap by utilizing third-party applications, but finds them unreliable and often perplexing.
4. **The complication**: What challenges does the antagonist create?
   Consequently, Mark lacks confidence in his data accuracy and campaign effectiveness.
5. **The protagonist's entrance**: Introduce your solution.
   Present [Your Product], an all-in-one marketing platform designed to simplify campaign management and provide comprehensive analytics.

6. **The journey begins**: How does your solution start addressing their needs?
   [Your Product] seamlessly integrates with Mark's existing tools, offering a unified dashboard for all his marketing campaigns.

7. **Obstacles overcome**: What hurdles does your solution help them clear?
   With [Your Product], Mark can now effortlessly track performance across multiple campaigns, eliminating the need for manual data aggregation.

8. **The turning point**: Highlight the moment when everything changes.
   Mark realizes he can now generate accurate reports in minutes instead of hours, revolutionizing his workflow.

9. **The climax**: Showcase the peak of their transformation.
   Armed with reliable data and efficient tools, Mark optimizes campaigns on the fly, significantly boosting engagement rates.

10. **The resolution**: Describe their new, improved state.
    Mark now confidently presents comprehensive reports to stakeholders, demonstrating clear ROI for all email marketing efforts.

11. **The lesson(s) learned**: What insights can be gleaned from this journey?
    Effective email marketing doesn't have to be a struggle; we've consistently proven this to be true.

12. **The new reality**: Conclude with authentic customer testimonials.
    As Sarah Johnson, Marketing Specialist at Global Innovations Inc., puts it: "Since implementing [Your Product], I've reclaimed hours each week. The platform's ability to consolidate data from various sources has given me complete trust in my reporting accuracy. It's been a game-changer."

This lighter framework and example answers can really help guide your team to producing a clearer more legible and believable story, something prospects can hear and relate to. Stay emotional and focused on the outcomes and you can incrementally improve sales and marketing results as long as the entire team tells the same story. But that's another matter altogether and is solved by alignment and sales enablement.

Finally, your value proposition. A strong value proposition is crucial for any business looking to stand out in today's competitive marketplace. It's the foundation of your business's marketing and sales efforts, clearly communicating your product or service's unique benefits and value to customers. A well-crafted value proposition can significantly impact your business's success by increasing conversions, boosting sales, and fostering customer loyalty.

Your value proposition helps potential customers quickly understand why they should choose your offering over your competitors, addressing their pain points and highlighting your specific solutions and differentiators. Moreover, a strong value proposition guides internal decision-making, aligning teams around a common purpose and ensuring that all business activities contribute to delivering the promised value. In short, a compelling value proposition succinctly articulates what sets your company apart. It attracts customers and helps retain them, ultimately driving long-term growth and success in the market.

To reaffirm, a well-crafted value proposition:

- Clearly communicates your unique benefits
- Differentiates you from competitors
- Helps customers quickly understand your offering
- Guides your marketing and sales efforts
- Increases conversions and sales

When you execute good positioning, messaging, and storytelling around a strong value proposition, you can't help but differentiate yourself in the market and drive more substantial market share. Try and shortcut this and its vanilla positioning, bland messaging and you may as well be hiding in the shadows. Blue ocean markets simply don't appear that much anymore, so you are in to win it, or you aren't, period.

Pillar #4: Pricing Strategy

Pricing strategy is key to customer acquisition and growth. You'll need to define your pricing strategy based on research and a solid financial model. This strategy includes pricing tiers, offers, discounts, renewals, and service level agreements. It also includes pricing models and a pricing framework that governs whether, when, and how you increase prices, if you allow discounts, and to what rates. If you are new to the market, please don't copy other pricing models, mainly because you don't know if your competitors have the most profitable pricing and aren't leaving money on the table. This is why you must research and speak to potential customers. Your job is to understand what value users, buyers, and decision-makers put on a solution like the one that you offer and price it accordingly. Don't get me wrong, in some industries pricing is pretty much standardized; tools like bookkeeping and accounting software are all pretty much the same. More complex tools have greater variance and an expectation of greater cost.

Example models include freemium, tiered pricing, custom enterprise, usage-based pricing, or combinations of these. Later in the book, we will discuss the various models and strategies and examine how product-led growth (PLG) companies approach pricing models compared to sales-led companies.

Pillar #5: Sales Enablement

Having a clear sales strategy is a must, and honestly, enablement is one of my favorite topics. I'm certified in both MEDDIC and MEDDPICC, sales qualification frameworks used widely in SaaS and fintech, as well as the Challenger Sales process. I'm saying that to win, you must begin with a sales method and a structured process that you can learn from and measure from the outset. These could also be BANT, SPIN, SNAP, NEAT, Sandler and so on. There's no point having all the tech and none of the practice, or as my dad says, "All the gear and no idea," which is often the case in startup environments. That's no slight to anyone, but rarely do startups hire highly experienced sales reps as they are budget-conscious and will try and find a self-imposed happy medium on skills and experience. Also they rarely hire people that can maximize the value of their tech investments, which is a fundamental flaw in their GTM. Tools like HubSpot are not platforms, they are products that are supposed to be custom built to your specific requirements, not off-the-shelf solutions. They can and must be customized, beyond the standard onboarding fee. I see so many companies skip over that to not maximize the value they offer. Your data is your power, so invest in it wisely upfront, not in retrospect.

For early-stage founders, just because you haven't sold your product doesn't mean you cannot map how the sales process might work. For example, if your product or service can't be put on a company credit card, assume it has to go through at least two to three decision-makers. In companies with a finance function, assume the finance leader has a say, too. Prep for multiple decision-makers and research these assumed influencers during your persona workshops and interviews. This way, you can learn something at all times and from all stages of your sales process. CRMs like HubSpot and Salesforce track how well email sequences perform. If you use their native calling functionality, you can track how conversations go, have calls transcribed, and keep a record of your best-performing sales calls. Even better, with HubSpot, you can define sales playbooks for the phone and listen to how reps execute them. And no, outbound calling isn't dead; some generations just prefer email. . .

Google Gartner's 2023 mock-up of the current B2B buying journey; the image lays it out plainly. The journey isn't linear, and there is no straight line to success anymore. As Donald Rumsfeld once famously said, "you have to cater for the unknown unknowns." Those are today's buying committees. Gartner recently published that there are up to 15 decision-makers in today's B2B buying process. Havard Business Review published a report that said for each decision-maker in a buying process of more than six people, the quality of decision-making deteriorated 10% per decision-maker. It is not surprising that around 40% of B2B deals end up with no decision being made.

So, design a sales process to fit around this style of customer buying journey (which takes marketing and sales alignment, by the way, so you have to do that) and plan for a large buying committee. If you have a plan from the outset, you can measure what is working and what isn't and continually optimize the sales process as you further understand your customers and prospects.

Build sales scripts, email sequences, objection handling playbooks, sales battle cards, a buyer funnel stages and tactics plan, cross-sell and upsell playbooks, product demo strategy if required, and sales confidence questions for your reps to tell you how well, if at all, this works. Implement a culture of continual training and learning so these valuable resources don't fall to the wayside unused—or worse—your sales team create their own (this is a big no) and run off gung-ho. Having a sales team that has been trained appropriately and is confident in their knowledge is an easy win and keeps the language consistent, avoiding messy messaging situations developing that damage your brand's perception in the marketplace.

Pillar #6 Marketing Tactics

I'm a proud marketing veteran, so this is a favorite area of focus for me. I've gone from funnel to flywheel. Although a funnel approach is considered outdated, you can still focus on awareness, interest, consideration, and decision-making content. For those more invested in a flywheel motion, the process aligns more with attracting, engaging, and delighting your audience, so HubSpot says. It overlays content to enhance the buyer and customer experience. In this model, nothing drops out of a funnel; you simply keep addressing your customers' needs across the entire lifecycle, pre-, during, and post-sale.

Have you ever seen companies constantly scrapping for new business? They are typically not that focused on retention and operate a funnel approach. It's always about the new business, not the upsell or cross-sell. Those focused on retention and upselling are flywheel adopters who keep spinning that flywheel until it delivers results (Figure 2.1).

Figure 2.1   Funnel vs flywheel approach to customer acquisition and retention.

Marketing tactics are varied and truly depend on the target audience. I've delivered inbound marketing, search engine optimization (SEO) on-page and off-page, account-based strategy, and paid advertising. These days, my expertise is delivered through strategic GTM planning, revenue operations, PLG playbooks, account-based marketing (ABM) playbooks, technical marketing campaigns, and partnerships. But that's because I like showing where I make impact, mainly in complex situations. I am a guy who loves a complex challenge, they excite me, put me under pressure and force me to find ways to solve them at scale. It would be a sad day when I opted for the monotony of a job that doesn't challenge me and bring out my competitive edge. We'll look at tactics in more detail later in this book.

Marketing holds the keys to your success. You can definitely sell your way to success, but it's rare these days. There is a constant battle for space in the mind of your buyer, competing with their everyday problems, personal life, social media, and more. Good quality, relevant, and timely content is how you get there and segmentation is king in my book, not content. Generic broad sweeping messaging isn't the way forward; segmented marketing that speaks to the micro communities within your audience is key. That's why brand and brand campaigns matter and are a must and lead gen sits underneath them. Brand buys space in the mind of your buyer and lead gen offers them a solution at the time of greatest need. They are two sides of the same coin.

Pillar #7: Onboarding and Retention

Onboarding is the place in the customer experience where most renewals are won or lost. I recently read some data from Akita App, a customer success platform, that said 74% of customers will switch to a competitor if the onboarding process is too complicated, and OnRamp, a similar platform, said 63% of customers consider the company's onboarding program when making a purchasing decision.

A poor onboarding experience can kill any type of longer-term deal, be that an upsell or renewal, no matter how hard you work to revitalize the relationship. Having an onboarding plan for those selling services or demo-based products is critical for understanding how quickly customers find and get to the value in your services or products.

Not only is it the onboarding, but the handoff from sales to customer success that still tanks widely in an age of automation. I mean, come on, do you really need to have large gaps in the process, or should we be triggering a seamless process from closed won deals in an automated workflow with CS or not? You tell me. I know the answer already.

Onboarding also lets you understand if it is appropriately planned and measured, how deep adoption goes, and the propensity to churn. It lets you learn signals across accounts that give churn indicators, like lack of use, lack of sign-ins, disconnections of other technologies like their CRM, for instance, from yours, etc. But how many companies don't even track these leading indicators?

By using automation, you can automate the upsell and cross-sell strategy based on product usage, and features users try to access to tie sales and customer success nicely. Again, more on this later. This part of the GTM strategy is wide open for reform.

Pillar #8: Product Development

Product is the final piece of the puzzle. What you develop, how you develop, and why you develop are critical to the long-term success of your business. I like to work by a simple set of rules around product development and answer a simple question once in the market: Did this feature or update we released drive more revenue, improve the user experience, or improve adoption?

If it does none of those things, why did you invest in it in the first place? Indeed, you can't be using a data-driven approach to product development if you did. If you use a data-driven approach, what did you learn from the data to help you strategically decide on features shipped or a pivot? Because let's be honest: a ton of products ship unwanted and unadopted features every year, and nobody gets penalized. It causes a lot of frustration across the company and with your user base, and it's time we grew with customer experience and revenue in mind from the outset. No time to waste really is the mantra of the day.

Connecting HubSpot directly to your product and creating a custom object for your product features to report on can work. Alternatively, you can use a product like Mixpanel and HubSpot to build reports showing what happens when a feature is released and how that impacts sales, marketing, customer experience (feature adoption), and revenue.

As you can see, this process builds a solid research-based strategy that aligns teams, focuses on the customer experience, and, as your flywheel spins, will improve the velocity of your revenue through closed won deals.

To Recap__

So there you have it. The eight pillars of GTM strategy clearly laid out for you to understand. Each pillar intrinsically valuable and tied to the next, often overlapping and entwinning for radical transformation and strategic success.

- Discovery
- Personas, Segmentation and Jobs To Be Done
- Positioning, Messaging and Value Proposition
- Pricing Strategy
- Sales Enablement
- Marketing Tactics
- Onboarding and Retention
- Product Development

PART

II

Overview of the ARISE Methodology

*"Go-to-market is the dominion of many and the expertise of few.
With this book I want to level the playing field."*

—Paul Sullivan

3

What the ARISE Go-To-Market Methodology® Is

ARISE IS AN acronym for Assess, Research, Ideate, Strategise, and Execute. Each stage of the ARISE framework is comprehensive. It's an approach wrapped around some of the world's most renowned research, sales, marketing, customer success, and product optimization frameworks and methodologies, my professional experience, and technology. It's an approach that now governs how I operate my consultancy and how that transcends into client delivery. It's also how you can win in today's competitive go-to-market landscape. Let's break it down.

- **Assess**: Gather the evidence and take stock of where the business is today.
- **Research**: Revisit your research and optimize it with our proven frameworks or undertake it from scratch.
- **Ideate**: Revisit your positioning and other crucial elements that impact your go-to-market strategy and suggest ways to optimize them for better results based on your research.
- **Strategise**: Map new goals based on the research's outcomes and ideas, building a new customer acquisition and retention strategy.
- **Execute**: Finally, agree on the road map for delivering the new revenue strategy, including tactics and timelines.

ARISE represents how firms can enable internal teams to onboard a new operating model. It's practiced, pragmatic, and practical. It doesn't require a large team to beaver away over a long time. It can be implemented and delivered in as little as a month, rapidly increasing ROI on the investment in technology, strategy, and, if you need me, the consultancy relationship. However, whether you speak to our team at ARISE GTM or follow the methodology outlined, you will still see varying degrees of success based on the accuracy of your research and available data. By continuing this flywheel approach, I'm sure you will see long-term incremental year-on-year growth.

The framework already considers the experiments it needs to run to ensure success, which means it anticipates how you can respond against unexpected market forces or underperformance. Not many agency or consultancy strategies can guarantee they've already considered most outcomes and how they can react based on the tactics they recommend employing beforehand.

Who the ARISE Framework Is For

The ARISE framework is for startups, scale-ups, and enterprise teams. It's a clearly defined and well-rehearsed best practice model that allows you to operate at the right speed, depth, and scale. It was designed and built for B2B product companies like SaaS, fintech, and technology-enabled consultancy businesses, but we've also proven the model to many service providers in the Business-to-Business (B2B) or Business-to-Business-to-Consumer (B2B2C) space.

When onboarding the ARISE methodology, I focus on best practices, concentrating on four crucial stages of your GTM:

- **Product Marketing**: How you plan to convey the value of your product to your best-fit prospects.
- **Sales/Buyer Enablement**: How you plan to enable your prospects to buy from you.
- **Customer Success**: How you plan to onboard, retain, cross-sell and/or upsell your customers.
- **Technology**: A clear understanding of the integrated technologies required to deliver an aligned GTM strategy with a 360° view of the customer.

This is the best-practice go-to-market approach, which ARISE is designed to do. We've made it an out-of-the-box GTM solution for teams that use HubSpot.

ARISE for the HubSpot Customer Platform

Given my passion for automation, I designed this approach to work on the HubSpot Customer Platform so it could work just as efficiently for Salesforce users. However, Salesforce has grown extensively by acquiring many products without native connections, so installing this may take much more work.

Because my team and I are experts in HubSpot, we've pre-built the ARISE framework into HubSpot with workflows, ticket pipelines, custom objects, event marketing campaigns, and, most importantly, key performance indicators (KPIs) and objectives and key results (OKRs) that can be deployed from the cloud. And the better HubSpot gets, the better your return on investment.

This means we can get HubSpot marketing, sales, and success teams live and onboarded on HubSpot in 48–72 hours. Within a week to 10 days, we can have your product data pushed into HubSpot with advanced reporting, enabling your business to have an accurate 360° view of your customers, enabling more intelligent customer acquisition and onboarding.

How ARISE Is Delivered

As with any program of work, ARISE has homework for preparation, immediate cloud-based deployment for instant ROI, and continuous improvement for customization and use cases.

Originally, a ticket pipeline called ARISE was installed in your CRM. Up to 84 tasks to complete the package you choose (standard, plus, or pro) can then be tracked for delivery speed and sign-off. Some tickets are timed to reopen to enable your teams to revisit elements of your GTM, like positioning, messaging, personas, etc.

Where needed, tickets have swipe files and frameworks attached for posterity, meaning you can revisit the work delivered repeatedly as your team or business evolves. This creates a success loop in a flywheel motion, which, as any HubSpot user knows, is a key reason for adopting it.

Now we deploy ARISE into a HubSpot portal complete with custom objects for strategic planning, competitive intelligence, customer intelligence, and battlecards for sales. Clients benefit from a wide range of pre-built resources within HubSpot, including 20 pre-built calling playbooks for various purposes, including case studies and objection handling. 33 email sequences for cross-sell, upsell, nurturing, and other key business processes and four key strategy playbooks for event marketing, developer marketing, customer marketing, and account-based marketing are also included.

As I said, we are currently building this as an SaaS application that utilizes HubSpot APIs to maximize intelligence and signaling, letting you, the CRM owner, use real-time insights to optimize your GTM approach. In short, I'm trying to make consultants and agencies redundant.

How ARISE Is Tailored for B2B SaaS, Fintech, and Technology-Enabled Businesses

Now, I want to give you background on ARISE and explain why I say it is specifically targeted at tech and technology-enabled businesses. It's because that's what I know. In my early career, it was all financial services—but tech-enabled projects littered my career, too. Post that time, it was e-commerce and apps and then fintech, insuretech, proptech, and real estate. Basically, I had a penchant for anything digital, hence my previous brand name, Digital BIAS. However, after the rise of AI, I found out that phrase has a whole new meaning, so I rebranded to ARISE GTM in line with the strategy.

Now that you have some background on my learned experience, you can see why I focused my attention and learning in these sectors. Running an agency or consultancy business myself, which is tech-enabled, and working with techpreneurs, as I like to call them, really inspires me to continue my journey. The pace of change and keeping up with that takes a lot; at the time of writing, HubSpot is shipping so many new features per month I doubt anyone truly knows how powerful the platform has become for anything longer than a few days at a time. What a time to be alive! It's fascinating how fast the tech landscape is changing.

Not meaning to divert your attention, my education has mainly been by tech firms on how to better run and build tech firms, except for the product marketing leaders course I took with the Product Marketing Alliance (PMA). That one was a game changer in the sense that I had all of this combined experience and expertise—tech development, web design, marketing, sales, and enterprise sales mixed with a deep passion for customer experience and success. When I took that course, the penny dropped, and I knew that my passion was go-to-market, comprehensively, not niche specialism. MEDDIC and MEDDPICC are both designed for selling tech products and if you look at my bookshelf, it's mainly product, sales, marketing, and philosophy, so I cannot wait to see this sitting up among my favorites.

So, to conclude, ARISE is tailored to B2B SaaS, fintech, and tech-enabled businesses because that's all I've known and been influenced by. What I have learned from building and shipping it is that it can be used just as successfully by service-led organizations if they are willing to put in the work.

PART

III

Assess

"If I had one hour to save the world, I would spend fifty-five minutes defining the problem and only five minutes finding the solution."

—Albert Einstein

4

Evaluating Your Current GTM Strategy

LET'S BREAK DOWN the ARISE methodology's assessment or "Assess" stage. In this stage of the process, you undertake a series of activities to take stock of where you are today. A large part of the assessment stage is understanding current performance, and to do that, you have to understand key performance indicators (KPIs) and how to use them.

As a business leader, I view KPIs as essential tools for evaluating the success of my organization, employees, and specific activities in achieving our key objectives. I use KPIs across various aspects of my business to assess operational effectiveness, track progress toward our goals, and identify areas where we can improve. The same approach is adopted when working with clients.

I've learned that KPIs must be both financial, like revenue growth or profit margins, and non-financial, such as customer satisfaction or employee engagement. For me, they serve as critical data points that inform my decision-making processes and strategic planning. To that end, I've found that knowing what to measure and when is crucial for driving productivity, maintaining objectivity, and fostering growth.

When I set KPIs, I ensure they're aligned with our strategic goals and follow the SMART criteria:

- **Specific:** I make them clearly defined and focused on particular aspects of performance
- **Measurable**: I ensure they're quantifiable and easy to track
- **Achievable**: I set realistic and attainable goals
- **Relevant**: I align them with our organization's objectives and strategy
- **Time-bound**: I set them within specific timeframes

In my experience, effective use of KPIs involves a mix of leading indicators, which help me predict future success, and lagging indicators, which reflect our past performance. By utilizing both types in my reporting, I can identify positive and negative patterns within our data and make more precise decisions for the future. KPIs help me and my team focus on what matters most, ensuring we allocate our resources efficiently and meet our strategic objectives. They provide me with objective evidence of our progress toward desired results, offering comparisons that gauge the degree of performance change over time. This approach has been invaluable in guiding my organization toward continuous improvement and success, so we have 151 KPIs as standard as part of the ARISE GTM Methodology®. I encourage you to start doing the same, if you haven't already done so.

Assessing Your Current Content

First, take a long, hard look at the content you have created and distributed to date. This should include sales, marketing, and any onboarding assets. Speak to your sales team:

1. To find out what materials (if any) have been centrally created.
2. To see who created their own materials and has stepped away from the rules or brand guidelines, if you have any.
3. What's being used and what isn't and why?

You should check call scripts, decks and presentations, proposals, quotes, emails, and event materials (in-person events) for sales teams.

Depending on your organization's size, there may be more than a sales team involved in this. For example, some companies have enablement teams separate from the sales team, and they may control this area.

You are looking for KPIs or metrics. The list below, which relates to the suggestions above, will provide some guidance; feel free to alter it for your use case. I go into more detail later in this book.

Call Scripts

Call scripts are really important, even for early-stage startups. They help reps build a process they can run and enable them to adapt it slightly to their style while ensuring they garner the information they need. Adopt a sales methodology that works for your company, and be mindful—there are at least 10 I can think of.

MEDDIC and MEDDPICC spring to mind as great qualification methodologies. However, you could consider the Challenger Sale, Gap Selling, and Jeb Blount's *Fanatical Prospecting* for outbound strategies. Look at your CRM for insights and heavily segment your customer data where possible. Below are some KPIs you can use to measure the impact of your content and assets:

- **Conversion Rate:** Measure the number of calls resulting in the desired outcome, such as scheduling a meeting or closing a sale. Use a CRM that has AI, records the transcripts, highlights the call's content, and tracks the sentiment and what is important to the prospect. Use that to prepare for the next call. Use the trends data to correlate buyer types, such as decision-makers, blockers, etc., and prepare your sales enablement strategy to combat that.
- **Average Handle Time:** Track the average duration of calls to ensure efficiency without compromising quality. Efficiency is not as important as results, but once you are getting results, you do need to optimize for efficiency. Lean into your trends data to inform your call strategy.
- **First Call Resolution (FCR):** Calculate the percentage of issues resolved during the first call, indicating effective

problem-solving. Again, with AI, use HubSpot's calling or Fathom.ai, Fireflies.ai; any of these tools from free to freemium will give you what you need. Use Fathom with HubSpot if that's your CRM.

Decks and Presentations

Sales enablement materials are another essential part of the sales process. Never let sales operate alone in this area as, in my experience, the wrong type of sales leader won't put enough emphasis on this, and reps end up creating their own decks, which means they are interpreting what's best about your product or service, rather than a centralized responsibility—led by marketing, who ensures that all materials are the same for everyone.

Consistency is key in the sales process, as you can end up with mixed messaging and a diluted value proposition that damages the revenue process rather than accelerating it. Decks can also be measured by ensuring that prospects are asked questions about the assets during the engagement process. Then, you should separately run internal NPS with sales reps on the quality of the materials to keep on top of their impact and validity.

Suppose you run a strong segmentation strategy within your sales operation. In that case, you should correlate how each segment most benefits from your product and alter your decks to each segment, emphasizing those features and benefits or desired outcomes first before moving into the wider product or service breakdown. Here are some KPIs you can use to measure how impactful your decks are:

- **Engagement Rate:** Measure how long prospects spend viewing each slide or section of the presentation. However, don't send decks out without presenting them first. Analyze the average time reps spend presenting a deck in a sales call—AI helps with this these days—and how many deals closed pre-use of decks and post-use of decks. Then look for closed won deals if/after any updates to your sales materials.
- **Completion Rate:** Track the percentage of viewers who go through the entire deck. The only way to do this is to use tech. Using the documents feature in HubSpot enables you to get a

signature via email and track how many pages that person or persons went through of your decks.

- **Conversion Rate:** Assess how many prospects take the desired action after viewing the presentation. The entire point of a sales process is to measure and refine; being deliberate is how you do that. It annoys me when the sales process is left to chance; how do you ever understand what works or does not?

Proposals and Quotes

Rule number one is never send a proposal without presenting it first. Then, as you learned from your sales decks, use a tool that enables you to track who else reads it by having to sign in to do so. If you can keep your tech stack slim and costs down, that's better for profitability, so choose a tool that carries digital proposals instead of sending something created in PowerPoint or Google Slides.

- **Quote-to-Close Ratio:** Calculate the number of deals closed compared to the total number of quotes sent.
- **Average Deal Size:** Track the average value of deals resulting from your proposals. Again, remember to segment your customers.
- **Time to Decision:** Measure how long it takes for prospects to make a decision after receiving your proposal.

Emails

Emails are still a key element of the customer acquisition process, and it's important to understand what you are measuring that has value and what supports vanity. Open rates are good, but so what? That could indicate good email subject headlines but not much more; open rates do not pay the bills, so optimize for responses first and then for the next stage; meetings, for example. Measure everything, waste nothing.

- **Open Rate:** Monitor the percentage of recipients who open your sales emails.
- **Click-Through Rate (CTR):** Track the number of recipients who click on links within your emails.

- **Reply Rate:** Measure the percentage of recipients who respond to your emails. This is your number one metric to measure. Emails need replies otherwise what's the point.

Event Materials (In-Person Events)

Every company should have an events playbook. First, create a strategy that ensures you attend events with the right target audience and have a clear objective and plan for each one. You'd be surprised at how many businesses sponsor and attend events and just see what sticks to the wall—spending tens of thousands for zero ROI.

I work with many companies that rely on collected business cards or the event visitors' registration tool, which can lead to problems with data. I've even seen the list of attendees sent to a sales team, but the sales leader didn't realize that they had it for three months. He then called the company and bad-mouthed them before they resent the original email from the previous quarter. It's not a situation to be throwing your weight around when your own house isn't in order.

I use HubSpot; I have a playbook with two or three iPads with forms that capture details and automatically enroll people in a 24-hour "it was good to meet you yesterday" email sequence. Great for attribution and segmentation, reducing reliance on reps following up manually and increasing the likelihood that any early open opportunities will engage in an expected timeframe.

- **Attendee Engagement:** Track metrics like session attendance, booth visits, or interactions with event materials.
- **Lead Generation:** Measure the number of new leads acquired during the event.
- **Follow-Up Conversion Rate:** Calculate the percentage of event attendees who convert into customers or take desired actions post-event.

General Metrics for All Content Types

If you have other forms of content not covered in this section, feel free to use a combination of the metrics suggested above or check out the list of KPIs at the back of this book. Below are a few more metrics that might work for this stage of the process.

- **Sales Rep Engagement:** Track how often your sales team uses each piece of content and run a sales confidence survey to understand how they feel about their performance.
- **Win Rate:** Measure the ratio of successful deals to total sales opportunities for each content type.
- **Customer Feedback:** Collect and analyze qualitative feedback from prospects and customers on the effectiveness of your content.

If you already have a CRM like HubSpot, you should be able to retrofit reporting to analyze most of this. Always remember to speak to people. GTP, Claude, and Perplexity are all good resources, but they should never be your oracle, at least not yet. Maybe in a few years, we'll have contextual AI, which will be a game-changer, but for now, we can use a combination of first-party data, tech, and people.

People will give you context, nuance, and vital information from earned insight that AI models don't have, and data is the record you analyze for truth. Always remember, sales teams are notoriously bad at inputting customer/prospect data, so I advise having a rigorous data entry process and regular cleaning to optimize your outcomes: bad data in, bad data out. Lastly, humans give you an emotional account, and how people feel about the tools and assets they're enabled with goes a fair way into how likely they are to adopt them. Speak to your team for feedback.

For the marketers reading, I'm sure you understand content performance reviews well enough, but some readers may be founders currently forced into the role or junior staff still finding out how they should approach this. I'd start by reviewing website messaging and copy, call-to-action performance, form conversions, landing page performance against industry averages, blogs, vlogs, videos, infographics, podcasts, webinars, etc., and any other materials you use. Again, if you're on HubSpot and utilizing the marketing and content hub, this is a simple exercise and should be purely data-driven.

Also, use this as an excellent time to talk to all marketing stakeholders and staff individually. You should try to understand the team's culture, such as whether there's freedom to contribute or if people are order takers from above. Creatives rarely work well in restrictive environments, and often, detractors can be the founders, so they need to know when to get out of the way. Here are some examples of metrics based on the examples above.

Website Messaging and Copy

- **Bounce Rate:** Measure the percentage of visitors who leave your site after viewing only one page.
- **Time on Page:** Track how long visitors spend engaging with your content.
- **Scroll Depth:** Analyze how far down the page visitors scroll, indicating content engagement.

Call-to-Action (CTA) Performance

- **Click-Through Rate (CTR):** Calculate the percentage of visitors who click on your CTAs.
- **Conversion Rate:** Measure the percentage of users who complete the desired action after clicking a CTA.
- **A/B Test Results:** Compare performance metrics between different CTA variations.

Form Conversions

- **Form Completion Rate:** Track the percentage of visitors who start and complete your forms.
- **Form Abandonment Rate:** Measure the percentage of users who start but don't finish filling out forms.
- **Field-Level Drop-Off:** Identify specific form fields where users tend to abandon the process.

Landing Page Performance

- **Conversion Rate:** Calculate the percentage of visitors who take the desired action on your landing page.
- **Average Session Duration:** Measure how long visitors stay on your landing page.

- **Bounce Rate:** Compare your landing page bounce rate to industry averages.

Blogs

- **Organic Traffic:** Track the number of visitors coming to your blog from search engines.
- **Social Shares:** Monitor how often your blog posts are shared on social media platforms.
- **Comments and Engagement:** Measure reader interaction through comments and discussions.

Vlogs and Videos

- **View Count:** Track the number of times your videos are watched.
- **Watch Time:** Measure the average duration viewers spend watching your videos.
- **Engagement Rate:** Calculate likes, comments, and shares relative to view count.

Infographics

- **Social Shares:** Monitor how often your infographics are shared across social platforms.
- **Backlinks:** Track the number of websites linking to your infographics.
- **Time on Page:** Measure how long visitors spend viewing pages with infographics.

Podcasts

- **Download Numbers:** Track how many times each episode is downloaded.
- **Listener Retention:** Measure how long listeners stay tuned to each episode.
- **Subscriber Growth Rate:** Calculate the rate at which your podcast is gaining new subscribers.

Webinars

- **Registration Rate:** Measure the percentage of invited people who register for your webinar.
- **Attendance Rate:** Calculate the percentage of registrants who actually attend.
- **Engagement Metrics:** Track participation in polls, Q&A sessions, and chats during the webinar.

General Metrics for All Content Types

- **Conversion Rate:** Measure how effectively each content type drives desired actions.
- **Return on Investment (ROI):** Calculate the financial return generated by each marketing material.
- **Net Promoter Score (NPS):** Gauge customer satisfaction and likelihood to recommend your content.

Again, these metrics are for guidance; you can and should expand them based on the maturity of your current strategies. To dive more deeply into your marketing, you can examine reporting, paid advertising, printed collateral, internal or external training, newsletters, marketing automation, lead nurturing, and PR. Let's look at some top-line metrics to focus your efforts.

Reporting

- **Data Accuracy:** Measure the consistency and reliability of data across different reports.
- **Actionable Insights:** Track the number of actionable recommendations derived from reports.
- **Report Utilization:** Monitor how frequently reports are accessed and used by team members.

Paid Advertising

- **Return on Ad Spend (ROAS):** Calculate the revenue generated for every dollar spent on advertising.

- **Click-Through Rate (CTR):** Measure the percentage of people who click on your ads after seeing them.
- **Cost Per Acquisition (CPA):** Track the average cost to acquire a new customer through paid advertising.

Printed Collateral

- **Response Rate:** Measure the percentage of recipients who take action after receiving printed materials.
- **Cost Per Response:** Calculate the cost of producing and distributing materials divided by the number of responses.
- **Brand Recall:** Assess how well recipients remember your brand after exposure to printed collateral.

Internal or External Training

- **Knowledge Retention:** Test participants' retention of key information over time.
- **Skill Application:** Measure how effectively trainees apply learned skills in real-world scenarios.
- **Training ROI:** Calculate the financial benefits of training compared to its costs.

Newsletters

- **Open Rate:** Track the percentage of recipients who open your newsletters.
- **Click-Through Rate:** Measure the percentage of readers who click on links within the newsletter.
- **Unsubscribe Rate:** Monitor the rate at which recipients opt out of your newsletter.

Marketing Automation

- **Lead Velocity:** Measure the speed at which leads move through your sales funnel.

- **Campaign Performance:** Track the success rates of automated campaigns across various channels.
- **Segmentation Effectiveness:** Assess how well your automated segments perform compared to non-segmented approaches.

Lead Nurturing

- **Conversion Rate:** Calculate the percentage of nurtured leads that become customers.
- **Time to Conversion:** Measure how long it takes for nurtured leads to convert.
- **Engagement Score:** Develop a scoring system to track lead engagement throughout the nurturing process.

PR

- **Media Mentions:** Track the number and quality of media mentions your brand receives.
- **Share of Voice:** Measure your brand's media coverage compared to competitors.
- **Sentiment Analysis:** Analyze the tone and attitude of media coverage toward your brand.

General Metrics for All Materials

- **Brand Awareness:** Measure changes in brand recognition and recall over time.
- **Customer Lifetime Value (CLV):** Calculate the total value a customer brings to your business over their entire relationship.
- **Net Promoter Score (NPS):** Gauge customer satisfaction and likelihood to recommend your brand.

Breaking Down a Website

While I covered a topline review of the website, I want to give you some tools that will help you do this more effectively, especially if your website is not on HubSpot's CMS and is on WordPress or a similar CMS. The tools I use to assess website performance are Screaming Frog, SEM Rush, Google Lighthouse, GTMetrix, and Pingdom. I'm mentioning these because they range from simple to complex, although there are more tools that you can use.

Screaming Frog The Screaming Frog SEO Spider is a powerful tool for conducting comprehensive website SEO audits. To audit small websites with less than 500 pages, start by downloading and installing the software, then enter the website URL you want to analyze. This can be done for free. The tool will crawl the site, gathering data on various SEO elements such as broken links, redirects, duplicate content, meta descriptions, and page titles. Note a paid license will allow you to audit much larger websites.

As it crawls, you can view and analyze the results in real-time, allowing you to identify common SEO issues like 404 errors, missing meta tags, and duplicate content quickly and efficiently. You can also use advanced features like custom extraction to gather specific data from web pages, integrate with Google Analytics and Search Console for additional insights, and generate XML sitemaps.

Once the crawl is complete, you can export the data to a spreadsheet for further analysis and to create actionable SEO recommendations. With its ability to crawl both small and large websites, Screaming Frog SEO Spider is essential for conducting thorough technical SEO audits and improving website performance.

One of my favorite tools is visualizing the website tree, which shows how the search engines read your website. If your website has all its pages clustered around the domain, you should find a professional SEO team to help you work on the website structure.

SEM Rush I love SEM Rush; some prefer Ahrefs, but I'll stick to what I know as I have limited experience with Ahrefs.

With SEM, you can dive into the details of the on-page and off-page SEO audit, learning which pages need further optimization, which pages might need to be scrapped, and what technical issues may prevent your site from ranking well.

If the issues are beyond your control, you can make many of the required edits and extract Excel files of errors to share with an SEO agency. I've taught myself a lot about SEO issues and can easily apply many fixes and rewrite the underperforming pages. You could likely use AI to support your initiatives around this. If you are bootstrapped, take the SEO courses they offer to learn the skills. However, SEM has been investing in its own content SEO tools, so you can leverage those as part of your subscription to enhance your marketing performance further.

SEM plays a bigger part in assessing your website and marketing performance. I utilize it for keyword research, domain analysis, competitor analysis, backlink tracking and more in the ideation and strategy phases. However, this tool should align with your growth strategy and flywheel loops to continuously improve website and content performance.

Five reports to set up in SEMRush are:

- Site Audit Report and track it weekly
- Domain Analytics report
- Traffic Analytics and connect Google Analytics 4 for accuracy
- Backlinks to track what you are winning and losing as they play a part in your search engine rankings

Google Lighthouse   This is a great site for measuring the performance of your website and how it loads in various environments from 3G to 5G and on mobile and desktop. Useful, but don't get hung up on it. Mobile scores are often low, and I always try to get them as high as possible, but if I open the site on a mobile device and it's loading fast, then track performance and listen out for more errors.

GT Metrix   This is an oldie but a goodie. It's very easy to run tests on various website pages and get a breakdown of how it loads worldwide and what causes the maximum load speed element by element. Often, you see how large images hamper your performance, and it's easy to swap them out with smaller versions. Other technical issues are also easily identified, but if you use WordPress, you'll notice that your plugins often add to your load speed, and you can't do much about those.

You can, however, jump ship and move to the HubSpot CMS where plugins don't exist; but hey, I'm not pushing an agenda here. You do what suits you.

Pingdom   It's another oldie, but again, it can be quite useful. When testing your website, use multiple sources to collect data. No one source is the oracle, so identifying trends is easier when you have multiple data providers.

What I like about Pingdom is that, like GT Metrix, it makes it visibly easy to identify problems with the pages you are testing and move to isolate and rectify them. The combination of these free, freemium, and paid subscription tools makes it easy for anyone to identify bottlenecks in the website and start correcting them.

Auditing Your HubSpot Portal

At the time of writing this, it became easier than ever to audit your HubSpot portals. It used to be a manual process, but more recently, a HubSpot partner built an audit tool that you can plug and play.

It breaks down your portals by level, pro and enterprise and analyzes usage, adoption, performance, and more. I'm not diving too deep into this but visit Portal IQ. You do not need a HubSpot agency to do this on your behalf; save a few hundred dollars and run it yourself. I use this tool myself if it makes any difference to your decision-making.

What you are looking out for is:

1. To prove ROI on your consumption of available features
2. Optimal use of automation, workflows, etc.
3. Adoption by teams
4. Opportunities to double down on use
5. What's working and what isn't
6. What other tools can be integrated into HubSpot

This leads me nicely into the next section on tech stack analysis.

Auditing Your Tech Stack

This activity is likely one of the most underrated in immature operations environments. The tech stack audit aims to understand what you
have, what is in use, and what can be removed, as well as to determine
whether it's the right tech stack.

With the CRM at the heart of the operational delivery of your
GTM tactics, the best stacks will be slim and integrated. In my opinion, I think there should be a centralized function for monitoring
SaaS subscriptions across the company rather than individual
departments running their tech budgets. Wouldn't finding three
separate internal teams or departments running the same tech waste
financial resources when an enterprise license would better suit
your purpose?

Smart GTM teams are fiscally responsible and budget-conscious
and look for slick integrations that do not require Zapier or Make to
make connections happen. That's not always an achievable outcome,
but it should be what you're working toward.

I remember being in the sales process with an ESG platform that
didn't communicate well, and there was a lack of understanding of
what tools were appropriate for what part of the business. I ended up
firing them in the sales process before the CEO called me back, and we
had a frank conversation about how the job is to deliver her strategic
vision and not to fight over what tech gets the job done. Needless to
say, the flags were there in the beginning, and we pursued the account
to an unsatisfying end six months later.

This is a note to you and myself: always listen to your thoughts; the
first ones are often right. Understand what tech should get the job
done, what is nice to have, and what is simply frivolous spending.
Here's an example of setting up a tracking sheet using Excel or Google
Docs. Each is a column header:

- App name
- Department(s) using it
- Billing owner
- Current role in the business process
- Total number of users
- Objective

- Metrics to track benefit
- Integrations with other apps
- Number of app integrations
- Total annual cost

Have this reviewed regularly, but always review it when you set your annual GTM strategy. The landscape changes so fast that you may find better tools at a lower price or that HubSpot has developed competing features natively to the Customer Platform.

Personas

A periodical persona review should be a standard for any revenue organization. It's not just a refresh but an ongoing process that, if scheduled, should be a quarterly review. You should run them all year round, build reporting against the most important and painful things, and track the validity of your messaging, sales outcomes, and customer success tickets to ensure the business solves them well.

By dedicating yourself to understanding how your customer behavior changes during your annual GTM strategy execution, you may find that you can identify markers that indicate when alignment slips. However, the days of selling yourself out of trouble at scale are slipping away, and every data point counts.

I'm a massive fan of personas and have a ton of valuable resources on our website at arisegtm.com. I've used them consistently, and if you've ever seen the persona property that HubSpot offers, you'll understand why, as we built ARISE into the CRM, we opted to create a persona object instead of continuing to use the native feature.

We developed a persona object because we wanted to make this a data-driven activity, and a custom customer intelligence object provides so much more flexibility and functionality. Add AI to the analysis and automation of data collection around personas, and you should be able to move your strategy forward in line with your buyers' changing needs.

Now that we have more in-depth data, we correlate the persona and the various stages of the decision-making process: awareness, interest, consideration, and decision-making. You can clearly show what content tactics will be used at each stage, and your AI can read these to help enhance your marketing and sales tactics.

I also want to highlight my use of the word tactics in marketing and sales. For the sake of continuity, GTM strategy means the business strategy and sales, marketing, and success have tactics to deploy the strategy.

It doesn't mean that sales and marketing don't have strategies, but that can become confusing to the reader, so I'll maintain my use of the language in this way.

A Documented Strategy

This is typically where I start seeing tumbleweeds. Many founders and business leaders don't have a strategy that is easy to find and is well documented. Less experienced agencies and consultants are often left wondering why they see results that are far from what they expected when they accept the strategy (tactics) the sales or marketing leader presents.

If you're doing your job well, you want to see the business strategy for the year so that you can pass your own judgment on whether or not what was presented would get the job done. Our job is not to simply accept what is presented but to dig deeper and align your thoughts with the wider business strategy. For example, if your CMO says, "We need to get to $4 million this year and here's my plan," how do you know if that plan will succeed? What did they benchmark their assumptions against? Based on previous results, what products will most likely help get there? What does retention and churn look like?

I don't mean you won't get there by failing to query it. Still, if you want to be seen as more than an order taker or content machine, you must prove your strategic nous and start asking the penetrating questions that can provoke uncomfortable conversations. However, by not probing, you potentially let both yourself and your client down, which is a problem.

I'm also not saying that agencies and consultants don't do a good job—far from it. There are some super-talented GTM engineers out there who deliver time and again. I am stressing that to review a current tactical game plan by your CMO or sales leader, you must correlate that to business strategy and the CRM data. The job is to discover where misalignment may have crept in and prescribe a remedial course of action if required.

Assessing the Teams' Skills

Right bums on right seats. You simply cannot win any other way. To reinvigorate your go-to-market approach, you must address the recruitment and talent in employment. No operational excellence or process optimization will solve the issue of carrying dead weight or having the wrong people in the wrong seats. It's one of the things we tried to address when we set up HubSpot. We repurposed CSAT and NPS into "temperature checkers" to track the sentiment of the workforce on a monthly and quarterly basis.

Why would you do that?

If you want to get into the data of an underperforming GTM strategy, the one thing a CRM cannot tell you is how the workforce has been feeling across the GTM lifecycle. As a founder and business leader myself, I want to correlate sentiment with performance, and this is a great way to do that.

When assessing an individual, it's extremely important to understand their drivers and desires, as people will always do best with what they're passionate about. You may find an underperforming sales rep is a better customer success rep. They may be better relationship builders than deal closers. It happens. Your job is to help flesh that out, and I can promise you one thing: if you try and handle this in-house, you may not get the truth from people as most will assume team leaders get the data, and they'll be fired or managed out. So, you can do a skills audit internally, or you can bring in a third party to run this part. Either way, it's an important part of any shift. You can also use this exercise to discover who else can help you perform your audit and rebuild your GTM strategy.

Assessing Product or Service Performance

Ask the marketing and sales team for evidence of customer retention rates, average lifetime value, average sales cycle length, average deal value, average monthly customer attrition, and revenue numbers. Collect this data to establish a baseline on which your new GTM strategy will build. Look for trends and correlations within the data to guide your more profound understanding of how your company's revenue machine works.

Companies should collect data on user segments from the product teams or, better still, send that data back to the CRM through an API connector or Mixpanel or something similar so that you can understand how who is sold to benefits most from what parts of the product. The product is the backbone of the company, and this is truly what drives revenue.

Reporting Performance

For the final stage of the assessment, you need to evaluate the current key performance indicators (KPIs) or metrics the business has been tracking. Identify what is being measured and why, what goals the reporting is designed to support, what was intended to be learned from the reports, and how that turns into actionable intent.

When done well, reports should make it easy for people to understand the next steps. We shouldn't need a data scientist to break down the data for us to execute against. Reporting helps you understand customer, prospect, revenue, and product user data. These four pillars are key to your long-term success, so make sure reporting dashboards tell stories, not reflect numbers.

When I First Ran ARISE on Digital BIAS

While writing this, I quickly looked at our historical data on pivoting my agency in the summer of 2023. During the assessment stage, we:

- analyzed 44 website pages (non-blog) and 151 blog posts
- fully analyzed the website from an SEO perspective
- audited our tech stack and lead scoring and our personas
- discovered our GTM was mainly in my head (poor showing there)
- assessed the team skills and made the necessary changes
- analyzed our reporting and KPIs

- ran a full competitive analysis on our six named competitors
- ran customer feedback and win/loss reviews
- reshaped our understanding of the size of the market
- rebuilt our positioning, messaging, value proposition, and story-telling frameworks
- Created five new products (services) from our service design workshop
- created a revenue operations model and strategy in Google Sheets from discovery to upsell for each product
- and launched a rebranded website

What happened was very interesting. We lost our web design business and the volume of business shrank because we shifted the GTM. I wanted bigger deals, more interesting clients and more technology building work. I achieved all of that.

I closed three deals in 2023 back to back—$160,000, $225,000, and $300,000. We had never closed deals of that size prior to the shift. Most of our deals were sub $125,000 and would renew; this was different. We also landed our first platform development gig for a fintech product in the US. In some ways, it was all I wanted, and in others, it was painful. We lost team members who were a part of the shift, and we never replaced them full-time. That created space for me to work with some fantastic senior industry experts, and guess what? That work has led me to refine our GTM further, write this book, identify the four key reasons why customers buy from us, build four totally different products, one for each customer segment, and hopefully, by the time you read this book, a new software platform. So, for all of you research naysayers, I'm telling you to buck your own trends and do the work; it pays dividends.

PART

IV

Research

"*If you don't ask the right questions, you don't get the right answers.*
A question asked the right way often points to its own answer.
Asking questions is the ABC of diagnosis."

—Edward Hodnett

5

Market Research Techniques

Primary and Secondary Research Methods

From my years of conducting market research, I've found that understanding the difference between primary and secondary research methods is essential for gathering comprehensive insights. Understanding the differences between the two will help you shape your research strategy with ARISE. Let me break it down for you and share some examples from my experience.

Primary research is all about collecting data directly from the source. I love primary research because it gives me fresh, tailored information specific to my research questions and the voice of the customer is absolutely vital to the long-term success of your business. Here are some primary research methods I frequently use:

- **Surveys:** I often create online questionnaires to gather quantitative data from a large group of people. It's a great way to get a broad overview of opinions and behaviors.
- **Interviews:** When I need in-depth insights, I conduct one-on-one interviews. These can be structured, semi-structured, or unstructured, depending on how much flexibility I need in the conversation.

- **Focus Groups:** Sometimes, I bring together a small group of people to discuss a product or concept. The group dynamic often leads to interesting insights that might not come up in individual interviews.
- **Observations:** In some cases, I'll observe people using a product or service in their natural environment. This method is fantastic for understanding user behavior without the bias of self-reporting.
- **Field Trials:** For new products, I might set up controlled experiments where participants use the product and provide feedback.

What's really valuable here is that with a CRM like HubSpot, you can use its integrated tools like forms and surveys, record telephone-based interactions, and use AI-connected tools like Fathom.ai for example to record calls outside of HubSpot, but ship that data back to the CRM. The question is, what are you going to do with it? Let it sit idle, or make it effective and poignant to your long-term revenue goals?

Secondary research involves analyzing existing data that's already been collected by someone else. I find secondary research incredibly valuable for providing context and background for our primary research. Here are some secondary research methods I regularly employ:

- **Literature Reviews:** I often include in a project reviewing academic journals, industry reports, and, if necessary, books related to our topic. This helps me understand the current state of knowledge in the field and gather any low-hanging fruit, although AI is definitely making this easier.
- **Government Data:** Many government agencies publish valuable statistics and reports. I frequently use data from sources like the U.S. Census Bureau or the Bureau of Labor Statistics in the US or data.gov.uk and the UK statistics authority here in the UK.
- **Company Reports:** Annual reports, financial statements, and press releases from companies in our industry can provide valuable insights into market trends and competitor strategies.
- **Market Research Reports:** Sometimes, I'll purchase reports from market research firms that have already conducted comprehensive studies in our area of interest.
- **Online Databases:** I often use databases like JSTOR or LexisNexis to access a wide range of academic and professional publications.

Research insights do not solely have to come from the person executing the research tasks. Gathering historical data and challenging perspectives can unearth a plethora of previously unconnected research and unconsidered possibilities when formulating a new strategic imperative. Secondary insights broaden your view of the landscape, whether or not your first-party dataset is small or large. By carefully selecting your data providers, you can aggregate that information into useable data points that can help prove or disprove your theories and speculations. But what other ways do we approach research using the ARISE methodology?

Tools for Market Analysis: SWOT, Porter's Five Forces, Win/Loss Interviews

As part of the eight pillars of go-to-market strategy, I cannot emphasize enough the importance of research and the application of qualitative and quantitative data.

Too early for product market fit? Use book persona interviews on respondent.io or wynter.com to get feedback on your positioning, messaging, and value prop. Oh, and don't forget pricing. Learn what value prospective buyers would pay for a product or service like the one you offer before leaving money on the table. Now, let's look at what research techniques we employ in ARISE.

SWOT Analysis in ARISE

The two most recognizable research methods and common frameworks are SWOT, which is applied to both your own business, products, and services and those of your competitors, and Porter's Five Forces, which again applies to both your and your competitors' companies.

If you don't already know, SWOT stands for Strengths, Weaknesses, Opportunities, and Threats. It's a straightforward yet powerful framework that I use to evaluate the current position of a business or product. Here's how I break it down:

- **Strengths and Weaknesses:** These are internal factors that we have some control over. I always start by looking at what we're/ it's good at and where we/it might need improvement.

- **Opportunities and Threats:** These are external factors in our business environment. I identify potential opportunities for growth and make myself aware of any threats that could impact our success.

What I appreciate most about SWOT analysis is its versatility. I can apply it to an entire organization or a specific product or service. It helps me gain a clear picture of where the business stands and where we could go. By conducting a SWOT analysis, I'm able to:

- Capitalize on our strengths
- Address our weaknesses
- Seize new opportunities
- Prepare for potential threats

In my experience, this comprehensive view is essential for making informed decisions and developing effective strategies. But remember, a SWOT analysis is just the starting point. The real magic happens when we use these insights to drive action and improvement. But how, you may be thinking, do I execute a SWOT analysis and align that with HubSpot, which is a CRM?

What's really exciting is how we can supercharge our SWOT analysis by integrating it with tools like HubSpot. This combination allows us to:

- Drive our analysis with real-time data
- Automate data collection for up-to-date insights
- Create custom reports that track SWOT-related metrics
- Align our marketing and sales teams around our strategic insights

Using our first-party data and not just a large LLM from OpenAI or some other equivalent, we can truly understand our landscape and establish a link between that data and our competitive landscape. We don't second-guess or overlook an AI hallucination, and we can be very confident that the answers to our problems, like it or not, are in our data and behaviors around understanding it.

Porter's Five Forces and ARISE

Next, Porter's Five Forces. As a business strategist, I've always found Porter's Five Forces analysis to be an incredibly useful tool in my approach, which is why I ingrained it into ARISE. Let me share with you why I find it so valuable and how I use it in my work.

Michael Porter, a brilliant Harvard professor, developed this framework, and I've come to rely on it to understand the competitive landscape of any industry or product. He focused on five forces that can impact an industry or product, in this case, to help you understand the likelihood of success or failure when launching a new product or service or optimizing a current one. These forces are:

1. Competitive Rivalry
2. Threat of New Entrants
3. Threat of Substitutes
4. Bargaining Power of Suppliers
5. Bargaining Power of Buyers

These forces are a solid anchor within the ARISE GTM Framework® and play a key role in my comprehensive approach to launching and sustaining successful products and services in the B2B space. The ARISE methodology (Assess, Research, Ideate, Strategise, and Execute) provides a robust structure for navigating the complexities of market entry and growth for both new and established products. What I find particularly exciting is how we integrate Porter's Five Forces into the Research phase of this framework. Let me share how I apply each of these forces in the tech industry:

- **Threat of New Entrants:** I always keep an eye on how easily new competitors can enter the market. For B2B tech, where innovation moves at pace, this insight is vital to critical decision making. I look at factors like entry costs, technological protections, and economies of scale.
- **Bargaining Power of Buyers:** In B2B tech, our customers often wield significant influence. I assess their price sensitivity, the number of buyers, and how easily they can switch to alternatives. This helps me tailor the value proposition effectively.

- **Bargaining Power of Suppliers:** From hardware providers to cloud services, our suppliers play a vital role. I evaluate their uniqueness and the costs associated with switching suppliers to understand our position better.
- **Intensity of Competitive Rivalry:** The tech landscape can be fiercely competitive. I analyze the number of competitors, market growth rates, and product differentiation to gauge how we can help you to stand out and differentiate.
- **Threat of Substitutes:** In the tech space, new solutions can emerge from unexpected places. I'm always on the lookout for alternative products or services that could fulfil your customers' needs.

What I love about this approach is how it feeds into the subsequent stages of the ARISE methodology. The insights we gain from Porter's Five Forces analysis fuel our ideation process, shape our strategies, and guide our execution. It also helps me see the bigger picture. It's not just about direct competitors; it's about understanding all the forces that can impact profitability and competitive position.

This is often overlooked or undercooked by early-stage founders, and I find it just as interesting for established companies, post-product market fit, when they don't have this information themselves based on research but an assumption of what the space looks like. That old "I don't wanna pay for research" mindset could actually be the very thing that's holding you back from growth. However, I also agree that nobody wants to pay thousands for pretty presentations anymore, without any execution on the back end of them.

Using Porter's Five Forces, I can help businesses identify potential risks and opportunities they might otherwise miss. It's an excellent tool for developing strategies that can give a company a real edge in its market, especially when revisited periodically.

Combining this analysis with other tools like SWOT creates a comprehensive understanding of our competitive landscape. This holistic view is invaluable for making informed decisions and optimizing go-to-market strategies. It's not just about understanding where you stand; it's about anticipating where the market is heading and positioning yourself for success.

This is exactly why if you're feeling stuck with your current go-to-market strategy, you should give the ARISE methodology a try. I've seen it work wonders, even in complex organizational environments. Remember, change can be challenging, but with the right approach and insights, it can lead to remarkable growth and success.

Win/Loss Interviews as the Rule, Not the Exception

Have you heard of win/loss interviews? They are a crucial part of the go-to-market process. They shouldn't only be used when you are reviewing your strategy but also as an ongoing method of staying attuned to your customers and their ever-evolving needs and buying processes.

Win/loss interviews should be run on as many deals as possible. The main reason is that unless you have a written rule on how your deals are registered as closed won or lost— that is, the reason they won or lost, you'll never understand your real-world performance; because reps are notoriously lazy in this department and they'll short cut the explanation. They don't want to overcomplicate the reason status. They want to keep it simple and easy to complete.

They don't often understand or care about the wealth of knowledge they can garner by undertaking the interviews either in person, over the phone or, in the worst-case scenario, by automated survey forms. However you collect this information, make sure that the reasons, call records, and form replies are curated into actionable intelligence that helps sharpen the sales process and immediately helps shape how marketing can talk to the different segments of your customers online with what matters to them. It's a critical cog in the flywheel for your business.

But it's not just about winning or losing; it's about understanding the entire decision-making process, and here's what I love about these interviews:

- They give us a clear picture of how our brand is perceived in the market
- We can spot gaps in our products or services that might be costing us deals

- They provide invaluable competitive intelligence
- We can fine-tune our messaging to really resonate with our target audience

And here's my structured approach you can adopt when you begin this process:

1. Carefully select a mix of recent customers and lost prospects.
2. Prepare questions that cover the entire buying journey.
3. Ensure the interviews are conducted by unbiased parties, such as someone like me, an external resource, or someone not from the sales team.
4. Analyze the responses to identify common themes and actionable insights.

In the resources section on our website that aligns with this book, you can find copies of example questions to help you get set up. Look for the links at the back of the book. Next, let's examine how win/loss plays a vital role in the ARISE® Go-to-Market Methodology®.

Integrating Insights into Our ARISE Framework

We weave insights into every stage of our ARISE methodology: Assess, Research, Ideate, Strategise, and Execute. It's all about continuous improvement and staying ahead of the competition.

Now, I'll be honest with you—implementing changes based on these interviews isn't always smooth sailing. When consulting with companies, we often face challenges such as internal resistance, prioritization issues, and resource constraints. But in my experience, the benefits far outweigh these costs, and it's best to persevere and be ready to make the business case. Change is rarely easy.

One tip I always share is the importance of getting executive sponsorship for your win/loss program. It's crucial for driving real change across the organization. I recommend starting with a small-scale pilot to showcase early wins and build momentum. Build allegiances with your customer-facing teams and, if present, your revenue operations team. Once you can articulate the benefits of your program, try finance and talk about the potential revenue benefits before bringing this to the wider C-Suite team.

Remember, you must start with the end in mind and have questions across all stages of the flywheel—awareness, consideration, and decision-making process. Here are some key areas I advise you to focus on:

- **Buyer Persona:** Understanding the role and responsibilities of the interviewee.
- **Brand Perception:** How and when they first heard about us and how their perception evolved.
- **Business Drivers:** The problems they were looking to solve and why they sought a new solution.
- **Selection Criteria:** The must-have requirements and the most critical factors in their decision-making process.
- **Buying Process:** How they evaluated providers and the key moments in their evaluation.
- **Competition:** Which vendors did they consider, and how do we compare?
- **Price:** The importance of pricing in their decision.
- **Sales Interaction:** Their experience with our sales team and any areas for improvement.

6

Competitive Landscape Analysis

Identifying and Analyzing Competitors

In the last chapter, I covered the different methods we employ to conduct research and analysis using the ARISE methodology. In this chapter, I want to examine the competitive landscape and how you must come to understand it. For example, a question you have to answer is: how do my prospects see my competitive landscape? The methodology allows you to access this information in several ways:

- **Win/Loss interviews:** As explained, win/loss is about understanding your prospects and customers' decision-making across the pipeline, and competitive decision-making is a critical part of that process.
- **Jobs-to-be-done:** While the JTBD framework is focused on what your customers are trying to solve by hiring your product or service, they must also discuss their decision-making and evaluation process, giving insight into how they decide on a particular resource.
- **Customer feedback:** By gathering insights from current customers, past clients, and even prospects who decided not to move forward, we gain a 360° view of our product's strengths, weaknesses, and opportunities.

- **Review websites:** Websites like G2, Capterra, Trustpilot, Reddit, and newer procurement-focused tools like Spendbase and Cledara can all help you identify your peers and competitors. Here, you can additionally gather insights from customers into what they like and dislike about your products, helping you understand third-party observations, reservations, and declinations.
- **Competitor logo interviews:** This is the most difficult of the set to engage. Start by scanning your competitor's website for the logos they display and reach out for a competitive interview. Pay for their interviewee's time and dive into what they are solving with your competitor's product. How long have they had it? What was the procurement process? Are they 100% happy with it, and why? If not, why not?

Essentially, research will make or break your go-to-market strategy, and while it's hard to maintain over long periods, using AI to revisit it frequently is a smart approach to solving this. So let's say you have completed the above, and you now have your list of competitor websites. What's next? Well, there's quite a lot to do.

First, you need to perform deep research into your competitors. Take time to focus on understanding six areas of their businesses, but remember to include your own business so you can clearly see the comparison when you revisit the completed work.

Analyzing a Company's Market Placement

Start by analyzing the position of the company in the marketplace. I start by identifying their intended customers, including various segments and industries. I look into how many clients they serve, noting that some businesses disclose this information on their websites while others might require more in-depth research. I also check if they have any major clients (logos) and which of these can be referenced for case studies. If they do, they usually highlight it prominently, making it relatively easy to discover. I then examine the countries where they operate to understand their geographical reach.

Additionally, I review their favorable online feedback to see what customers appreciate and contrast it with the criticisms found in negative reviews. It's important to note any drawbacks mentioned even in their top reviews. Including excerpts from some reviews along with their star ratings can provide deeper insights. Finally, I look for noticeable patterns in their online complaints and observe how these patterns have evolved over time to get a sense of ongoing issues or improvements.

Analyzing a Product or Service

Next, analyze the product or service. I start by comparing the range of products offered by both my client's company and their competitors. I then examine the key features that define these products and consider what value they bring to customers or the outcomes they aim to achieve. Pricing is another critical aspect; I compare how much we charge versus our competitors and look into any current discounts or promotions, especially those offered in enterprise sales scenarios. Understanding their perceived strengths and weaknesses helps me assess their market position, hence competitive SWOT and Porter's Five Forces. I also check if they offer free trials or pilot programs, which can be a significant factor in attracting new customers.

Then, I investigate any partnerships they might have, as these can enhance their market reach and credibility. To understand how their customers access support, I look for where they provide help documents and articles. If I have access to their user experience, I break down its pros and cons to see how it compares to our own/client's offerings. This comprehensive analysis helps me understand the competitive product and/or service landscape and identify areas for improvement or differentiation for my clients or my own business.

Analyzing the Positioning

After looking at the market placement and then analyzing the products and services, I look at the positioning of the business. When analyzing a product's positioning, I begin by examining how the company differentiates itself from others in the market. This involves looking at the unique features or services they offer, as well as any niche markets they target. I then review their messaging strategies to understand how they communicate their value proposition, such as highlighting specific benefits that address customer pain points or using testimonials to build trust. It's also important to identify the use cases they have listed, which can provide insights into how their products are applied in real-world scenarios.

After this, I pay attention to how their messaging might vary across different customer segments or industries, such as emphasizing affordability for small businesses or scalability for enterprises. This comprehensive approach helps me understand the company's market positioning and how effectively they communicate their strengths to different audiences. This information will help you understand how you can work on your own differentiation in your new GTM strategy. Next let's look at assessing the public facing marketing strategy.

Analyzing How Companies Communicate

When I'm evaluating a product's public marketing strategy, I begin by identifying their tagline if present to understand the core message they want to convey. I then assess the level of activity across their marketing channels, such as blogs, social media, webinars, eBooks, emails, podcasts, and newsletters. I might even engage by signing up to their marketing content to stay attuned to their news and updates. This helps me gauge their engagement and reach.

Next, I analyze the types of content they prioritize on their top three channels—whether it's thought leadership, practical how-tos, or product-focused material. Understanding their marketing approach is crucial; it helps me determine if they target the industry broadly or use account-based marketing (ABM). I also explore the topics they discuss and the keywords they bid on to identify any emerging trends that might indicate new developments.

Engagement levels are another important factor; here, I evaluate how effectively they engage with their audience on different social media platforms like Facebook, Twitter, LinkedIn, Instagram, and TikTok. Additionally, I review what they're communicating in press releases, paid campaigns, and events.

Partnerships can also play a significant role in their strategy, so I look into any collaborations they have. If they host or attend events and trade shows, this can offer insights into their networking efforts. Comparing their organic search rankings to ours provides a benchmark for SEO performance. Lastly, I assess their website's visual identity to see if it aligns with current branding trends and check for any interactive tools or recent competitions that could enhance customer engagement.

All of this can indicate, but not solidify, what's working and what isn't. For that you have to correlate the content types with your own audience and owned channels. What you can learn here is where new opportunities lie; for example, where your audience is accessible with TikTok.

It's a lot so far, but keep with me here. I always say nothing's worth doing if you don't do it properly, and I've got two more areas to cover to wrap this up.

Analyzing Sales and Customer Success

When I'm analyzing a product's sales and service strategy, I start by examining its sales process to understand the steps it takes to convert leads into customers. I also look at the length of their sales cycle to see how quickly they can close deals. It's important to know if they offer live chat or chatbots on the website to communicate with sales or customer service and what the customer experience is like with these tools. Partnerships are another key aspect; they can be used in many different ways in a go-to-market motion, so I identify any collaborations they have and with whom. I evaluate the types of sales assets they use, such as presentations or product sheets, which can often be found online or through insights from new hires who previously worked for competitors.

Understanding their response time for customer inquiries is crucial; reviews or complaints often highlight if it's exceptionally good or bad. Additionally, I investigate how they handle and escalate customer complaints to ensure issues are resolved efficiently. Use review sites for finding this detail if you haven't yet found this on their website or with quick searches. Also include non-typical places for research like Reddit, where product users also congregate to share painful tales of company performance, good and bad. This comprehensive approach helps me assess their effectiveness in sales and customer service, providing insights into potential areas for improvement or competitive advantage.

Finally, but not comprehensively, you want to get an understanding of the company's history. When I'm analyzing a company's history, I start by looking into any recent acquisitions they've made or if they've been acquired themselves, focusing on deals from the last three to five years. This helps me understand their growth strategy and market positioning. I then assess their growth trajectory to see how they've expanded over time. Understanding the size of their workforce is also important, so I break down the number of employees by major departments to get a sense of their organizational structure.

Furthermore, I also examine where their support and sales teams are located, as this can impact their operational efficiency and customer service capabilities. If any departments are experiencing a hiring surge, it could indicate areas of expansion or increased demand. Lastly, I consider the words that best describe their customer-facing teams, which often reflect the company's values and approach to customer service. This comprehensive analysis provides insights into the company's strategic direction and operational strengths.

Using Competitive SWOT Analysis

Now that we've completed a run-through of the competitive analysis process in the ARISE go-to-market strategy, let's move into competitive SWOT. As advised in the last chapter, we analyze the strengths, weaknesses, opportunities, and threats of each competitor. You should find overlap in the results at an industry level, but you are looking to identify the feature and benefit level data to understand how you differentiate. Then use that information in your marketing strategy and sales enablement materials like battle cards or your outbound compete strategy email sequences. Let me give you more guidance on how you approach each stage when running SWOT for your own business:

- **Strengths:** From everything I've identified in my competitor analysis work, what are the standout areas where I excel beyond my competitors? You might consider aspects like hosting highly engaging webinars, having a team of exceptionally skilled professionals, offering an outstanding mobile application, or achieving significant customer traction.

- **Weaknesses:** Conversely, where did I fall short compared to my competitors? It's important to acknowledge that every business has its weaknesses, whether it's in areas like customer service, response times, missing features, or low SEO rankings. Here's a tip: as I evaluate my strengths and weaknesses, I make sure to consider not only the actual ones but also those that are perceived by others. Think jobs-to-be-done research.
- **Opportunities:** Based on your competitor and customer research, what trends or untapped markets are emerging that you could jump on? This could be anything from a new feature or market to press opportunities. Also, remember to look for areas of the business that can be optimized to open up/capitalize on an opportunity.
- **Threats:** What could get in the way of your success either right now or in the future? Think about things like new competitors, a change in regulations, new technology, a shift in customer needs, areas where customer servicing costs can spike, etc.

This may feel like a lot of work, and it is; there's no escaping the fact that this work is hard, takes time, and is still open to human interpretation of what's important and what is not, hence my extensive guidance in this respect. Research must probe every possible aspect, but in a very targeted way and that is why we use well known and respected frameworks to perform research in ARISE.

Creating a Competitive Matrix

Guidance is a key part of the strategic process. Just sending people out to execute tasks rarely produces anything of worth, unless they are experienced in the subject matter, but more often than not, juniors are tasked with research because senior professionals deem themselves more useful elsewhere. Personally I think that's an incorrect decision process as your experience is exactly what separates you from AI and those less experienced who will likely use it to perform said tasks. This is where a competitive matrix comes in handy.

Creating a competitive matrix is part of my competitive analysis process, allowing me to visually compare my strengths and weaknesses against competitors. I start by identifying both direct and indirect competitors. Direct competitors offer similar products or services, while indirect competitors satisfy similar customer needs with different offerings. Next, I determine the evaluation factors by choosing key performance indicators (KPIs) relevant to my industry. Common factors include product features, pricing, market share, brand reputation, customer service, and innovation.

Once I have my evaluation factors, I gather accurate and up-to-date data for each KPI from reliable sources such as market research reports, industry publications, and customer feedback. With this data in hand, I construct the matrix by creating a grid with my company and competitors listed on one axis and the evaluation factors on the other. This can be done using tools like Microsoft Excel or Google Sheets. I then assess each competitor based on the selected factors and assign ratings or scores for each criterion to reflect their performance.

After evaluating the competitors, I populate the matrix by entering the ratings or scores into the corresponding cells. This visually represents the strengths and weaknesses of each competitor compared to my organization or the one I'm working with. I analyze the completed matrix to look for patterns, trends, and insights. This helps me identify areas where my company excels or needs improvement and recognize competitor advantages that can be leveraged or mitigated.

Using the insights gained from the matrix, I develop strategies to inform strategic decisions, such as pricing strategies, product development, marketing tactics, and overall business positioning. There are different types of competitive matrices that I might use depending on my needs. A feature comparison matrix allows me to compare product features across competitors to identify unique selling points and gaps in offerings. A SWOT analysis matrix helps me evaluate strengths, weaknesses, opportunities, and threats for each competitor. A competitive profile matrix uses weighted scoring of critical success factors to benchmark against competitors. Lastly, a competitive positioning matrix plots companies on axes representing key success factors to highlight strategic positions in the market.

By following these steps and utilizing the various types of matrices, I can gain a comprehensive understanding of my competitive landscape and make informed strategic decisions to enhance my market position. Now, I'm sure you are starting to understand why the ARISE framework delivers results. Its comprehensive nature enables agility, responsiveness, and decision-making at speed at all levels of the organization cross-functionally, which proves its adoption across both revenue and product teams, while clearly informing strategic decision-making at the C-Suite level.

7

Customer Insights Gathering

Methods for Gathering Customer Feedback

There are numerous methods for collecting customer feedback from face-to-face interviews, AI agents, forms, surveys, net promoter score (NPS) surveys, customer satisfaction (CSAT) surveys, product/feature usage data, support tickets, feature requests, product user video recordings, in-app feedback surveys, social media listening, online review sites, testimonials, case studies, focus groups, and old school lunches and dinners. There are a lot of ways, and they can all be equally useful and impactful. The social levers here, such as lunches and dinners, don't necessarily need explaining, but the other methods are worth discussing.

Again, I am going to come back to HubSpot here as my favored CRM and customer management platform as you can create multistep interview forms, integrate with a tool like Typeform for a customized onbrand experience and, going back to HubSpot, use the built-in calling functionality to record interviews to customer records. Again, with the rise of AI inside HubSpot and, at the time of writing, knowing they plan to open their CoPilot up to custom objects, the storing of all this research and analysis there in your CRM can and will become the difference between winning and losing, which again is why we are building Leevr, our own AI GTM strategy platform for teams on HubSpot.

It takes the ARISE GTM Methodology®, digitizes it and then uses your first-party CRM data to optimize the entire GTM workflow.

So, on to gathering customer feedback and its methods. Manual or automated, feedback is vital to businesses to understand their audience, improve user experience, and make informed decisions. It also gives you the information you need to keep your organization a customer-centric one. Let's look at some of the examples and why you should adopt them:

- **Face-to-Face Interviews:** These provide deep insights through direct interaction, allowing for follow-up questions and observation of non-verbal cues. In the ARISE GTM Methodology®, they help build personal connections and trust with customers.
- **AI Agents:** AI agents can efficiently handle large volumes of feedback, offering quick responses and analysis. They enhance the scalability of feedback collection. The downside is that I don't think we are quite ready to be interviewed by AI agents just yet.
- **Forms:** Forms are versatile and can be used to collect structured feedback at various touchpoints across the customer lifecycle. They facilitate organized data collection that informs decision-making.
- **Surveys:** Surveys gather quantitative data that can be easily analyzed for trends. They provide measurable insights into customer satisfaction and preferences.
- **Net Promoter Score (NPS) Surveys:** NPS surveys measure customer loyalty and likelihood to recommend a product. We use them in ARISE GTM to understand brand advocacy, product and service value, and correlation with churn.
- **Customer Satisfaction (CSAT) Surveys:** CSAT surveys assess immediate satisfaction with a product or service, offering actionable insights.
- **Product/Feature Usage Data:** Analyzing usage data reveals how customers interact with products, highlighting popular features and areas needing improvement. This data-driven approach supports strategic decisions in ARISE GTM.
- **Support Tickets:** Support tickets provide direct feedback on issues customers face, helping improve customer service and product reliability.

- **Feature Requests:** Gathering feature requests helps prioritize development based on customer needs, aligning product offerings with market demand.
- **Product User Video Recordings:** Video recordings offer visual insights into user interactions, identifying usability issues and enhancing user experience within ARISE.
- **In-App Feedback Surveys:** These capture real-time feedback during product use, providing immediate insights into user experience that drive continuous improvement in ARISE GTM.
- **Social Media Listening:** Monitoring social media captures spontaneous customer opinions and trends, aiding brand reputation management.
- **Online Review Sites:** Reviews provide candid customer opinions that influence potential buyers and inform product improvements in ARISE.
- **Testimonials:** Testimonials highlight positive customer experiences, serving as powerful marketing tools within ARISE GTM to build credibility.
- **Case Studies:** Case studies showcase successful use cases, demonstrating value to potential customers and supporting sales efforts.
- **Focus Groups:** These provide qualitative insights through group discussions, uncovering deeper motivations and preferences that guide product development.
- **Old School Lunches and Dinners:** Informal settings foster open dialog and relationship building, enhancing customer loyalty and understanding.

So, in the context of the ARISE GTM Methodology®, these methods collectively contribute to a comprehensive understanding of customer needs, preferences, and experiences, enabling more informed strategic decisions and fostering stronger customer relationships.

My advice is not to try and do all of these at once. Segment your current customer base into groups based on common characteristics such as industry, product purchase, product usage, or whatever makes the most sense and move them through different feedback loops over time. Of course, the other part of this is that some intended recipients may have their preferred methods of communication, too. All in all, this comprehensive list of feedback options can be used as part of a long-term data improvement strategy and help you implement a Voice of the Customer (VOC) program.

Analyzing Customer Behavior and Preferences

Once you've collected all of this information, you need to break it down into actionable intelligence. First, let's start by recognizing that understanding and analyzing customer behavior and preferences is instrumental in shaping effective go-to-market strategies, especially in the context of the ARISE methodology.

Customer behaviors are the actions and decision-making processes of your customers and prospects as they interact with your products and services. Recognizing these patterns allows you to tailor your offerings to meet their needs more precisely. In the ARISE framework, understanding customer behavior is integral to each stage, from assessing incumbent strategies to executing new ones. The gained insight directly influences purchasing decisions by helping you craft compelling value propositions and messaging that resonate with your target audience.

Moreover, it guides the overall GTM strategy by ensuring that every element, from product development to marketing and sales, is aligned with customer expectations, driving long-term sustainable revenue growth and amplifying your competitive advantage. Also, when analyzing customer behavior, several key factors come into play, each influencing how customers interact with products and make purchasing decisions.

- Personal factors such as demographics, lifestyle, and personal goals and experiences shape individual preferences and buying habits.
- Psychological factors, including perception, motivation, and beliefs, drive how customers perceive value and make choices.
- Social factors like family, culture, and social networks further impact behavior by shaping norms and expectations.

Understanding these elements is crucial in the ARISE methodology as it allows us to tailor strategies that resonate with our target audience's unique needs and desires, which ultimately enhances the effectiveness of our go-to-market efforts. This is why extensive persona interviews are a key part of the process and why I advise that you record them in your CRM. By analyzing the data at scale with AI, you can find trends, spot shifts in customer behavior and education about your product, industry, or sector and learn when they see alternatives to your product or service enter the market.

Map Your Customer's Journey

Mapping the customer journey is another essential process for understanding customer behavior within the ARISE framework. The customer journey encompasses several stages:

- awareness,
- consideration,
- decision-making,
- and post-purchase evaluation.

By mapping this journey, we gain insights into how customers interact with our brand at each touchpoint. This understanding enables us to create targeted strategies that guide potential customers smoothly through their journey, addressing their needs at every stage. Within the ARISE methodology, customer journey mapping is essential as it aligns our strategic efforts across all phases: Assess, Research, Ideate, Strategise, and Execute, ensuring that your go-to-market strategy is both comprehensive and customer-centric. So, what could these touchpoints look like?

Well, to start, consider that there are online and offline touchpoints, or digital and physical, however you prefer to label them. I'll list some examples so that you can tie activities to stages of the funnel:

- **Online awareness:** Paid advertising (PPC, display ads), online PR, social media
- **Offline awareness:** Print media, radio, TV, word of mouth, events
- **Online consideration:** SEO, paid advertising, email marketing, paid search, landing pages, website, social media, third-party review sites, communities, Reddit

- **Offline consideration:** Direct mail, events
- **Online decision-making:** Forms, demos, self-serve products, freemium models, case study
- **Offline decision-making:** In-store, leadership meetings, peers and colleagues
- **Post-purchase online:** Surveys, NPS, CSAT, email, loyalty programs, upsell, cross-sell, knowledge base
- **Post-purchase offline:** Call center, offer in invoice, postal mail

Each company has its own unique variation on the above, and it's your job to remain curious and not accept what you believe to be the status quo. Finding out small, useful snippets of information can still grow revenues by percentages, and you must always win percentages. Compound results often bear more fruit than large one-off wins, so please get to know your customer's journey segment by segment to set yourself up for long-term success.

PART

V

Ideate

"The biggest room in the world is the room for improvement."

—Helmut Schmidt

PART

V

People

8

Brainstorming Innovative GTM Approaches

IN THIS CHAPTER, we look at brainstorming. But in truth, I'm not a massive fan of ideation through random action and undefined objectives. In the B2B space, everything we do must be deliberate. Intent is key for growth; anything else is playing at business and I don't have the time or inclination for that. So, in the process of the ARISE methodology, brainstorming covers this.

- Service design
- Redefined value proposition
- Redefined positioning
- Redefined messaging
- Redefined storytelling
- Confirmed jobs-to-be-done

In the previous chapters, I have gotten right to the processes we use in the ARISE GTM Methodology®. We've broken down what we do and why it's important.

I want to start with service design. It's fundamental to creating a new go-to-market strategy as it forces you to be honest and transparent with your business and look to move to a customer-centric business model.

How I Used Service Design

In 2023, when I wanted to move my business from a traditional agency model—you know the one, basically a smorgasbord of agency services in a website—to a product-led model, it forced me to look deeply into the business and expose the frailties, misadventure, and misunderstandings of my audience. I had to answer a question: "How do you experience an agency, without talking or engaging with the team there?" To answer this question, I designed a service design workshop. To begin with the team researched all of the challenges our target personas faced and then broke them down into three columns.

- What we can solve with a product or service.
- What we can solve with marketing content.
- What we can't solve at all or is too far removed from our sphere of influence.

This helps you understand how you can help the personas at hand and where you shouldn't waste any time. This can then help your product or service development and define where to focus your content marketing efforts. In some cases, you can also work out who you need to target for partnerships as alternative routes to market. In total, we identified 92 different challenges across 5 personas, which gave us a lot of insight into who has the biggest challenges as we enter the world of AI. These were Customer Success, Product Owners, and Chief Technical Officers, followed by your Chief Revenue Officer and then your CMO.

Personally, I have identified more personas, but I tend to segment by function and seniority rather than build 8, 9, or 10 separate personas. The reason I adopted this approach was to avoid over complication of the segmentation and also to reflect that different companies have different titles executing the same roles and functions.

The service design workshop required me and my team to answer the following questions and tasks, I suggest you stop the book here if you haven't already performed a workshop like this before and collectively bring your marketing, sales, CS, product, and operations teams into a one-day workshop and run through it.

1. Identify the ways in which a user can find the product or service
2. List the names (words, terms) a user can use to find our product or services

3. How do we set the users' expectations or outcomes of our services?
4. How do we enable the user to achieve their goal?
5. How do we create a familiar process for the user?
6. How do we break it down into easy to understand language?
7. How do we enable our champion to sell us internally?
8. What are the minimum steps to completing the service?
9. How do we create a front-to-back experience?
10. How do we ensure no dead ends?
11. How do we ensure that anyone can access our services?
12. How do we create consistence among users and staff?
13. How do we consistently update our processes with market forces?
14. How do we create a decision-making process?
15. How do we ensure that human assistance is available at the right time?

If you can objectively and truthfully answer these questions without inherent bias or reverse engineering answers to your current status quo, you have a huge opportunity to redefine your organization as a truly customer centric one. We identified:

- 15 different ways we can be found online
- 150 plus keywords and search terms
- 5 job (JTBD) outcomes (one for each persona)
- 8 different ways someone can ask the same questions to a search engine
- 22 different ways to manage user expectations
- 14 different ways to enable the outcome
- 16 different aspects to combine to create a familiar process
- 11 ways to keep the language easy to understand
- 12 ways to enable our champion
- 29 different ways for a user to get quick time to value from us
- 19 different ways to keep the experience consistent front to back
- 15 ways to avoid roadblocks in our products or services
- 10 different ways for always on access to learn about our business or get support
- 9 ways to keep a consistent human experience
- 6 ways to keep our processes fresh and updated
- 11 steps to keep decision-making consistent
- 7 ways to keep human assistance available at the right time

And this is just one part of what I put together to create the ARISE methodology. This Service Design process isn't mine; it's adopted and adapted from Lynn Shostack's *Harvard Business Review* article "Designing Services that Deliver" published in 1982. What I have ensured is that service design does not sit squarely in the realm of product development, but is a tool the company adopts to completely shift its GTM momentum. If this looks like a lot of work, it is; going to market is hard and I'm about done with hearing how "I don't think all of this is necessary." Go tell Gartner and query their 2023 GTM report that found that 70% of all GTM strategy fails because of internal misalignment.

And if I am honest, RevOps is a plaster developed to cover the cracks in poor operational growth strategy fueled by a mantra of raising your way out of trouble and founders ducking out of instilling best practice. It's completely needed, but as with a lot of new things, it's really just a rerun of an old black-and-white movie. For years industry grew on best practice and yet in the event of a boom, it all gets thrown out of the window for profits. Hopefully those days are slowly coming to an end and fiscal and operational responsibility will take pride of place again in the boardroom. However, in regard to RevOps, HubSpot is doing a great job building a platform that allows customer facing teams to use a single tech stack to support a collective GTM approach.

Leveraging Research Insights to Generate Creative Solutions

A key resource in any go-to-market motion today is artificial intelligence (AI). I've mentioned this already in the book, but it needs more focus. Using it to help you shape your thoughts from the research you've been performing is absolutely the right use case. I hate people who don't use their first-party data or research data to underpin the use of AI. Even in my own team, I always call out the use of AI without any of our data being used. Think about personas, historical sales patterns, best-performing marketing and/or sales assets, best-performing blog posts, our proprietary ARISE methodology, etc.

Combine your first-party data with data that has strong credentials from tier-one resources, and you can extrapolate some really strong ideas for marketing, sales, and product development strategy. For example, our ARISE methodology has around 84 swipe files to help execute the process through a project management tool, and we now use the questions and guidance within these files to support and execute the ideation process. We also have earned experience around the execution of the methodology and, therefore can spot information that is out of place or unexpected.

Let me tell you how I created our four killer products for our 2025 go-to-market strategy. First, we ran a CRM analysis. We analyzed the closed won and closed lost deal records and the questions asked and answered during the sales process. This starts with forms, chat conversations, surveys, and the win/loss interviews we successfully undertake with data stored in custom properties in our CRM. This analysis enabled us to understand why our customers came to us. This broke down as follows:

a. 60%—startups with an underperforming customer acquisition process inclusive of marketing and sales
b. 20%—scaleups needing a revenue operations solution
c. 10%—enterprise companies needing an account-based strategy
d. 10%—enterprise companies spinning out a new product as a startup

Armed with this clarity, our proprietary GTM methodology, and a new partnership with a company that builds web apps from Figma designs and AI, we first completed the storyboarding exercise. We then uploaded this to Perplexity.ai and created a value proposition and positioning statement. We added historical sales data and our persona profiles to create a killer offer for each ideal customer segment based on data. From here, we ran SWOT and Porter's Five Forces across the killer offers and a segment hypothesis to look at our revenue opportunities.

Again, we layered in more queries, uploaded previous marketing and sales campaign data, and then asked Perplexity to suggest a sales strategy. When we got the first set of revenue numbers back, which was based on the total available market, we added our team size and some other factors to the calculations, reflecting our target markets:

1. Seasonal fluctuations in B2B sales
2. Holiday periods in both the UK and the US
3. Typical slow periods for B2B sales

The recalculated data was then adjusted as below:

1. **Q1 (Jan–Mar):** Typically slow start, post-holiday recovery
2. **Q2 (Apr–Jun):** Generally strong for B2B sales
3. **Q3 (Jul–Sep):** Summer slowdown, especially in August
4. **Q4 (Oct–Dec):** Strong finish, but holiday season can affect B2B sales

To include these additional considerations;

1. **UK-US differences:** The UK typically has more concentrated holiday periods (e.g., August), while the US has a more distributed pattern.
2. **Industry variations:** B2B SaaS, fintech, and management consultancies may have different seasonal patterns.
3. **Economic factors:** The projected economic challenges for 2024 might affect spending patterns.
4. **Flexibility:** The program should be adaptable to accommodate clients' schedules around holiday periods.

I'll leave you to explore this further for your strategies. Remember, this search and exploration required our CRM data and no gaps; we didn't run queries on data we did not have ourselves.

Tools Incorporating AI

2024 saw a rapid increase in the integration of AI into a raft of startup and enterprise products, some of which made sense and some did not. I think those who find it most difficult are companies like HubSpot because the product is designed to be customized to unique use cases at a per-business level. Therefore, its AI has to be useful but not coercive. Adobe Photoshop, on the other hand, provides AI that can help accelerate your graphic and image design outputs. Now, I'm not saying Hub-Spot's AI doesn't accelerate the adoption of its product suite because it does. Still, at the time of writing they have some way to go before partners can tap into its AI Application Programming Interface (API), making it easy for partners and developers to fully own the end-user experience. This creates a great opportunity for companies to build low-cost GPT assistants and models that only help that specific company optimize their GTM from all of its data.

However, because GTM requires multiple data points, typically from multiple data sources, I foresee the biggest opportunity is to consolidate the performance of multiple sources or products and services into one single product—tools that leverage and enhance the tech stack instead of adding further complexity and integrations.

Claude from Athropic just launched its ability to log in and run software on your behalf, which is a crazy indicator of where the landscape is going. In the long term, it could be a cost-effective way for companies with complex tech stacks to operate them without ripping everything out and starting again.

For now, I would only use AI with your first-party CRM data, any third-party research, and the prompts from the resources we developed for ARISE, or, of course, those you are happy using internally. It's a short stop on AI, but I also feel like I'd like to revisit AI-led GTM in 2026, potentially as another book looking at a more mature landscape.

9

Exploring Channel Strategies

Direct Sales, Partnerships, and Digital Platforms

As we approach the final part of the ideation process, we should consider the different ways you can take your business to the next market. To get started, you can consider what channels you can best exploit including marketing channels, direct sales, partnerships, and, of course, digital products.

By now, you should have amassed enough data by following the process to discover plenty of opportunities to revamp your go-to-market strategy. If you completed the service design workshop, you should have done enough research on your customers and the competitive landscape and have a better outlook on how you can better serve current and future customers. Armed with this, the potential is exponential. So, let's dive into channel strategies.

Marketing Channels

Marketing channels are well known across the B2B lifecycle. From paid advertising to advocacy programs we pretty much know where we can operate, but not always why we should operate. Many companies often run into the tactical execution game without the context or nuance of foresight or foreplanning, at least not the right planning.

The B2B customer acquisition process is now more complex than ever before. And you see the industry shift with the prevailing winds, rehashing old playbooks and polishing them up like a pair of new shoes, styled slightly different but ultimately still the same thing. Let's break a few of them down.

Inbound Marketing

Inbound marketing has become an essential tactic for most companies looking to establish a strong go-to-market strategy. This approach focuses on attracting customers through relevant and helpful content rather than interrupting them with traditional outbound marketing methods.

As today's buyer has become more internet savvy, they increasingly seek content that addresses their needs and provides value. Some 70% of buyers are well educated about their problem before they enter into a buying cycle. This shift in behavior has made inbound marketing particularly relevant for companies as it aligns well to the sales cycle.

At the core of inbound marketing is the creation of high quality, targeted content. This can include blog posts, ebooks, webinars, video, and social media content that speaks to the different stages of the buyers' journey. If you can provide your prospect with valuable, problem solving information, you can establish your business or those representatives of your business as thought leaders people trust. By optimizing that content for search engines, you bring organic traffic, although the organic game is under pressure from AI and search engines fighting for relevancy. Social channels have developed beyond LinkedIn, X, and Facebook to Reddit, Instagram, and TikTok, challenging companies to find ever more useful ways of engaging with their audiences and meet them where they are.

Finally, lead gen. Inbound has been lead gen focused for some time as its multi-medium approach focuses on capturing and nurturing leads through offers like free trials, ebooks, and webinars. These approaches provide value to potential customers while allowing companies to collect contact information for further marketing efforts based on email automation.

Benefits for B2B Companies

1. **Customer Retention:** Inbound marketing helps build long-term relationships with customers, which is crucial for tech and service companies relying on subscription models.
2. **Cost-Effectiveness:** Compared to traditional outbound marketing, inbound strategies often provide a higher return on investment.
3. **Targeted Approach:** By creating buyer personas and tailoring content to specific audience segments, SaaS and fintech companies can attract more qualified leads.
4. **Measurable Results:** Inbound marketing strategies are highly trackable, allowing companies to continually analyze and optimize their efforts.

In today's marketplace, inbound is being replaced with demand generation, which is basically inbound marketing with paid advertising.

Demand Generation

This is another term I playfully tease. Demand generation. The very idea that the term stands for seems ludicrous to me. Demand capture I understand. In digital channels people who are looking for products or services can be captured; in no circumstances can they be generated. You cannot prompt someone to look for something they have not yet identified they need, especially if we accept that the average buyer is between 60-80% of their way through researching a solution before they reach out. However, for companies with a broad target audience, undefined addressable market, unknowing of the revenue opportunities available to them, this strategy makes sense. In reality demand generation is a name for digital marketing. Look at what it entails to see this for yourself:

- Identify your target audience
- Use content and paid advertising to attract and educate the target audience on your products or services
- Capture interested parties and convert them into leads

Demand gen focuses on awareness and brand building and so is very much an awareness play, whereas lead generation is about converting brand aware prospects into paying customers. If you take a strong look at HubSpot's Inbound Marketing Playbook, it contains both pieces of this puzzle rather than separating the two. Demand generation uses tactics like obtaining organic website traffic, event registrations, social media interactions, newsletter sign-ups, and content downloads, whereas lead generation uses tactics like lead scoring, form submissions, product-led growth tactics, free trials, and other conversion tactics. Ultimately, you use both in tandem to best acquire new customers, enter new markets, build brand awareness, and drive sales pipeline. For me these two are closely aligned by application.

Product-Led Growth (PLG)

Do you think PLG is something new or something rehashed and updated? Do you believe free trials are new or rehashed? Do you think freemium is new or rehashed? Let me tell you, freemium has been around since the 80's in the form of MS-DOS shareware games Blox and Crux. Even when Wes Bush created the PLG community and course, which I attended in all fairness and worked on as a consultant, I called it out as not the silver bullet solution silicon valley and the VC/PE landscape did; feel free to connect with me on LinkedIn and scroll through my historical posts. To be clear, this isn't suggesting that I called Wes out, just the idea that PLG was the new savior; it's always been another optimization channel to be included in the mix. Kyle Poyar, who also hugely backed PLG for a number of years and is widely considered the PLG guru and someone you should follow, has recently gotten behind the account-based approach to customer acquisition, which we will get into shortly.

What you'll also see in my historical posts is that I called PLG an optimization channel and not much more; and to a degree I was right, but not entirely. PLG has a place in your GTM under the right circumstances but most PLG companies still run outbound sales motions. What I do love about PLG is that it commits the organization to building a better customer experience and that in itself is worth the consideration. While the products are quick to access, they are also quickly punished if the user experience doesn't match the user expectations. Check out the PLG resources on the website through the links in the back of this book. PLG playbooks usually consist of ongoing freemium access models with flat rate or usage-based pricing with a heavy focus on quick time to value. Think Canva, Slack, and products like this.

Account-Based Marketing (ABM)

Can I start by saying that this space is currently the most annoying. I love the ABM approach but can we leave it as just that. Why we have Account-Based Everything, Account-Based Experience, Account-Based Approach, Account-Based Sales, can we stop with the naming conventions; they are totally unnecessary, and it feels like they do more to help the creators into the history books than they do for the practice itself. That being said, let's get into this one.

Account-Based Marketing has been around for decades; the practice first appeared in the early 90s although the Information Technology Services Marketing Association (ITSMA) coined the term in 2004. During the 2010s it gained popularity with the first ABM courses and certifications as well as the first marketing automation and ABM platforms. I wanted to stress the importance of knowing the history of ABM so you don't get caught up in the latest wave of it. Again, check my posts on LinkedIn; I have been calling out ABM as good go-to-market—it has alignment, collective customer experience focus, deep understanding of the target accounts is required, it's everything you want. Pretty much like ARISE, it's deep, broad, and thorough. In my opinion, whether you are an up market or down market tool:

- You can only serve a certain amount of business in any given market in a geolocation
- This means you should be able to find and name the companies that are available to you
- Which means with the tools available to you today, you don't need to waste marketing and sales budget on spurious, uneducated, ill-informed customer acquisition playbooks. You can directly target those accounts with location based or LinkedIn profile based ads, content marketing, direct mail rather than PPC (Google Ads).

- You can even use tools that tell you when companies exhibit buying behavior online with tools like Bombora, SimilarWeb, Clay (this I know the least about) and so on. You've even got tools like RollWorks, 6sense, DemandBase, Terminus, and N.Rich ABM platforms that help strategies with intent data and the ability to target tightly with ads.

The idea that you can define who you can sell to, in many cases identify what technology that they already hold or have held, see how the company is performing departmentally and as a whole, and adopt tools that help you do this and then deliver you the contact details, means if you add all the work you would have undertaken by following the book to now, you would have a robust GTM for the future. GTM isn't hard, it's just competitive and the competition is constantly learning new methods and approaches, rehashing old plays and calling them something new, or just lurching into every fad trend that pops up, but you shouldn't. You should analyze your current situation, research how the industry is currently receiving products or services like yours, delve deeply into what makes your customers buy from you as well as recommend you to others. Then brainstorm how you can use those learnings to drive ideas for your forward strategy, before planning as we are now on how you can execute it. Now you can see why ARISE makes sense. Again for readers, check out the ABM assets and strategy docs in the readers' portal on the website.

Direct Sales

Direct sales have taken a nosedive over recent years, especially telesales. The advent of email changed how we communicate, and rather than email becoming a tool that you use to reconfirm agreements and send documents, we used it as a channel for all. We try to close deals with emails to audiences that don't know us, and we try shitty tactics that infer the recipient's time isn't valuable, like "I haven't heard back from you. Can you tell me if you are (a) too busy, (b) not interested, or (c) bad timing?" I'm sure you have received an email of this type before. If you sent one, shame on you.

What else gets me about this is how we try to circumvent sophisticated sales processes with largely spammy behavior. First, we introduced rules to prevent spam, then we decided to move from the email inbox to LinkedIn inbox and spam people there under the guise of LinkedIn marketing, and now so-called sales experts are telling you to buy lookalike email domains and spam your audience from there because it's getting harder to connect. One key reason you fail to connect is that the average inbox now receives so many emails we just tune out. Standard email-based direct sales is now more luck than judgment. However, it still has a role to play, as does LinkedIn.

In fact, if I were putting a playbook together, I would have a platform like Dripify for LinkedIn and run upfront relationship building campaigns there. I would connect with my personas, share related content, and engage with their posts and content before moving to a sales-based conversation. Use the research to provide content topics that should resonate with your audience and slowly share content that introduces your product or service. But in today's market, that is still not enough. You have to be more clever. You need to use multiple channels and "signals" to understand your audience and when they are actively in the market. Bombora intent data is now in most GTM tools you buy, enabling you to see which companies are showing intent around particular topics related to your business. G2 can tell you if companies you may be targeting are researching companies that look like yours, and they also use Bombora data to enhance that experience. LinkedIn data is widely scraped to look for growth signals in your target business verticals, such as headcount, revenue growth, demographics, and more. Combine these signals with your first-party CRM data, think form fills, social media engagement, and website page visits, and you can start to understand which of your target accounts are in play. More on this to follow.

Coming back to direct sales. The phone seems to be an outdated medium for some, yet I think it has to be a cornerstone of your outbound sales strategy. I'm not talking about buying unsolicited lists and cold-calling people, but using your signals and calling when the moment seems right makes perfect sense. You can use email and LinkedIn messaging strategies to target prospects who score low on engagement or lead scores to increase your value proposition's visibility and generate some demand. Calling, email, and social media messaging make sense if your business is a demo-led sales organization, but if you are a product-led or freemium-offer organization, focus more on email, social media, and paid advertising. It's not as cut and dry as that; as I said, if you've followed this guide, the answers are in the work you've done in the Assess and Research phases.

Partnerships

Next up are partnerships. This is always a bit of a grey area. HubSpot has nailed its partner program; I recently read that it contributes some $29 billion in its annual revenues each year, and that's growing. But even the best partnership programs come under fire; consider WP Engine, a WordPress hosting solution program that ended up in a battle with the very product it sought to leverage. It wasn't the partnership program itself that was targeted. WordPress called an infringement on its trademark with WP Engine, and the outcome of this could directly impact the partnership program.

Strategic partnerships, however, should always be considered. For example, I partner with a headhunter who recruits leadership teams in fast-growing tech firms. He refers me to incoming leaders, and I quickly overcome the stranger gap. I am also a HubSpot agency partner, among other things, and that partnership helped me curate the ARISE GTM Methodology®. Other partnerships, like the one with RollWorks, a US-based account-based marketing platform, led me to work with Direct Sourcing and Heidi and Amit, a company we will discuss later in this book.

Partnerships for tech and service firms have always been a strong GTM channel. The right brand, shared target audience, and complementary services or products all strengthen a value proposition. Financial benefits like the ones HubSpot partners receive help sweeten the deal, but the best partnerships help both parties grow their respective businesses. What I've seen fail in the partnerships space is when in SaaS and fintech companies, they are treated as indirect "direct" sales channels; that is, partnerships are extensions of the sales team, not independent bodies with their KPIs and revenue goals.

Far too often, companies forget that partners often hold a relationship with their customers, and they don't leverage those relationships easily. It's worse when the partner manager asks the partner to find five or six of their own clients to open conversations with. In my experience, the best partnership programs work because the targeting is correct. The company correctly identifies their target partner, much like a persona or ideal partner profile, and understands how it can help that partner drive value for their customers beyond adding another tool or product to the tech stack. They have a co-marketing and branding program, can co-sell on the right opportunities, build value in the relationships for the long term, and use tiering to help. Ultimately, a partner program is part of the business's long-term growth strategy and isn't a 6–12 month "try-it-out" approach. If I were setting up a partner program, I'd also look at using products like Partnerhub, Partnerstack, Reveal, and CrossBeam to build my partnership program and bring verified partners to me.

Digital Platforms

Throughout this book, I've constantly referred to digital platforms. You can't run go-to-market without tech, and there are a number of ways to use tools to enable yours. For example, how would you enable a community program if you were to build it? You could use Slack or a dedicated product like Mighty Networks, Circle, or LearnWorlds, depending on what works for your audience, as that is the key to community success.

Then, you have CRMs like HubSpot, Salesforce, or Pipedrive. My preference is for HubSpot, but budgets can drive your tech choices. Collecting owned data has never been more important to you than the world we are living in and moving into—more governance on collecting and obtaining data, the rise of artificial intelligence and its ability to analyze data in real-time and provide trend analysis and other key insights.

Your website content management system, the integration of plugins, modules, website themes, and more all count toward the cost of your go-to-market strategy. If I were in a super early stage, I'd use a marketplace like Themeforest to buy a $60 WordPress theme and spend time optimizing my positioning, messaging, storytelling, and value prop before investing in any large-cost custom design. More often than not, your website's look and feel are subjective and less obstructive to the sale as the prospect lacks understanding of what you offer by what they read.

A marketing tool is a prerequisite for any structured GTM approach. Marketing automation is a must for sustained campaign success using segmentation, lists, landing pages, newsletters, forms, calls-to-action, social media management, ad management, basically everything you need to run successful customer acquisition campaigns. Again, like many others I use the HubSpot marketing and content hubs to seamlessly manage my campaigns because of the combined data I collect by also hosting my company website on the CMS. By visualizing the customer journey across my CRM, CMS, and social channels and tracking customer and prospect behavior and interactions, it helps build that first-party data set for ongoing analysis and improvement.

Customer success platforms are also a crucial part of your GTM tech stack. I use HubSpot service hub and custom-built my own portal, which you, as a reader of this book, can access for supporting materials. There are, however, many dedicated customer success tools to choose from. Last but not least, there is a product analysis tool. I like Mixpanel, but you have Pendo and other tools designed to help you understand who and how your product is best adapted. Tracking product usage data and shipping that back into your CRM is how you win in GTM. Cross-reference your front-end CRM segments with your product user-segments and you will soon learn how to communicate your product or service's value to each customer segment. But always remember you have to build your GTM plan and then choose the tech to enable it.

The biggest transformation to the go-to-market tech stack is AI. The opportunity for progression, rapid development, and the scaling back of the number of tools in your stack seriously increased. Anthropics Claude just announced that it can access software on your behalf which has set the tone for how AI will impact recruitment, future tech adoption, and the creation of highly reduced reliance on multiple tools. I foresee supertools that grab multiple sources of information and optimize across the customer acquisition lifecycle. HubSpot has introduced Breeze.ai which is their first step into accelerating the GTM process in this direction, but I also see the drawbacks for them as they need to maintain a platform that is customizable for each owner's use case rather than moving into a shaped product offering a directed solution. However, the future is definitely bright in this space.

PART

VI

Strategise

"The thing is, continuity of strategic direction and continuous improvement in how you do things are absolutely consistent with each other. In fact, they're mutually reinforcing."

—Michael Porter

10

Developing a Clear Value Proposition

HEY, WE ARE into the final straight from here on in. Now we can get into strategy and execution, which is the exciting part of GTM, right? Throughout the book, we've leaned into understanding your current position, being naked to the truth of your current situation, researching the landscape and your customer base for more answers and insights and then using that information to start some big blue sky thinking. You're doing well. Now it's time to get tactical, and we will kick Strategy off with developing a clear value proposition. To begin with, answer the following questions:

- Who specifically buys your product and why?
- What problem do your customers buy your product or service to solve?
- How do these users explain that your product solves their problems?
- Why did they tell you that your product or service differentiates from the competition?

Write these answers on a whiteboard or somewhere you can look up and see them while you work on the rest.

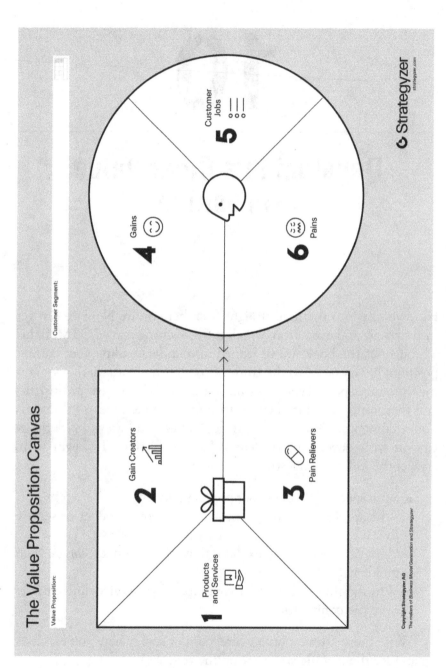

Figure 10.1　A Value Proposition Canvas

Define Your Value Proposition

Defining a value proposition isn't that hard. There are a ton of resources available, and like most, we employ the Value Proposition Canvas by Strategyzer. I actually have a 6 ft. whiteboard at home that has one drawn on one side, with the business model canvas below it (Figure 10.1).

To help us break this down, please note the numbers 1–6 added to the canvas so that I can explain the purpose of each section. On the left-hand side of the canvas, you will list where you discuss your product/service and the gains from its use or the pains it solves.

Value Proposition

1. **Products & Services:** This section identifies the product or service you are offering to your prospective customers.
2. **Gain Creators:** In this section, list the benefits that your product or service offers your ideal customers.
3. **Pain Relievers:** In this section, list the pain relievers that your product or service offers potential customers.

On the right-hand side of the canvas, you discuss the product from the perception of your customer segment or persona.

Customer Segment

4. **Gains:** List how your product or service provides gains for this customer segment.
5. **Customer Jobs:** List everything your potential customers have to do to feel the gains and relieve their pains.
6. **Pains:** List all of your customer segment's pain points.

Note that you should now have all the research on hand to help complete this quite quickly. Having a data driven value proposition based on how your customers tell you they experience your product or service and the outcomes it enables can quickly move you into a more productive sales and marketing strategy.

Characteristics of a Great Value Proposition

As a rule of thumb, there are 10 characteristics of a great value proposition. These are:

- They are embedded in great business models
- Focus on a few pain relievers or value creators, but do so
  extremely well
- Focus on jobs, pains, or gains that a large number of customers
  have or for which a small number of customers are willing to pay
  a lot of money
- Align with how customers measure success
- Focus on the most significant jobs, most severe pain points, and
  most relevant gains
- Differentiate from the competition in a meaningful way
- Address functional, emotional, and social jobs all together
- Outperform competition substantially on at least one dimension
- They are difficult to copy
- Focus on unsatisfied jobs, pains, and gains

If you can ensure that your proposition meets all of these standards,
you can maximize the potential of your product or service's positioning
within the marketplace for increased deal flow and brand recognition.
However, this isn't the only thing you need to ensure your business's success.

Testing the Value Proposition

Based on the various courses and reading materials I've read and taken
on the subject, once you create your value proposition, you need a way
to test it. First, you can answer the following questions:

(1) **Is it tailored to a particular customer segment, or is it too
broad to be effective?**
    Avoid generalizations. You must pinpoint the specific
industry, company size, and key challenges. Generalities won't
cut it; you're aiming for precision.

(2) **Does it prioritize the customer's perspective? Is it tailored to their needs?**

Does the message revolve around your product or service offerings, or does it directly address the customer's pain points?

(3) **Will it strike a chord with the intended audience? How can we be certain?**

This is where market research becomes crucial. You need evidence that this value proposition truly resonates. Have you gathered feedback from at least 10 in-depth qualitative interviews and potentially hundreds of quantitative surveys?

(4) **How does it set itself apart from competitors, including the option to maintain the status quo?**

Differentiation is key. Clearly outline the current situation, including the "do nothing" scenario where customers acknowledge the problem but hesitate to invest in a solution. Sometimes, your biggest rival is inaction—people settling for "good enough."

(5) **Does it come across as authentic?**

Is the message trustworthy?

(6) **Does it evoke an emotional response—can customers relate to it on a personal level?**

I often encounter value propositions that are overly technical and full of buzzwords. While that's fine, remember that emotions often drive the buying process. In the cybersecurity realm, for instance, fear is a significant motivator. While you shouldn't explicitly mention fear, it's crucial to recognize that IT professionals and CISOs are concerned about potential breaches. Other emotions like excitement, empowerment, or confidence might be relevant. Incorporate these emotional elements into your value proposition.

(7) **Does it use language that customers understand, avoiding industry-specific terms?**

We often fall into the trap of using jargon, especially in B2B tech companies where acronyms abound. Strive to use words that resonate with customers. Be mindful of this.

(8) Is it straightforward, persuasive, and believable?
Finally, does it convince? Is it trustworthy? Is it easy to grasp? Your message testing should confirm these aspects.

Now that you have answered these questions, you can contact your customers and prospects and conduct interviews to obtain additional information and confirmation. Again, we have a number of resources for this on the support website for readers; see the back of the book.

11

Creating Messaging Frameworks

NEXT, WE WILL focus on redesigning the messaging to be in line with your findings. We need to establish a framework for doing so. It should contain the following elements:

- Your new value proposition
- The target audience
- A short written version of the value proposition in less than 30 words, if possible
- A broader, more expansive explanation of the value proposition
- Your brand tone of voice
- The top 1–5 outcomes from your research per target audience
- The differentiator you established from your research
- The top 1–5 pain points your product or service actually solves
- The information on how well your product or service solves the pain points and what features give that benefit
- Success stories or case studies

As you read through this you can clearly see how you can build messaging around outcomes, pain points, and feature benefits, enabling you to cover prospects that buy from any of those perspectives. In my opinion, there are at least 15 different ways you can communicate product or service value without choosing particular distribution channels. Consider the number of channels your research told you to operate in, and you could expand that to 6× or 7× quite easily. Take in that there are around 40 or so content types you can use in your marketing and sales strategies, and you can see how your GTM transforms.

Build Your Messaging Framework

If you have come this far, then you have all the necessary ingredients to build and test some robust messaging frameworks. To begin my work, I like to use Perpelxity.ai, yes AI, to give me some concepts. The way I get there is to upload a persona profile, including all of the work just completed, and the URL for a product or service on your website, and ask it to build you five or ten messaging frameworks for each persona. I then review them and see what makes sense and what's simply buzzwords and no substance. This approach is good for accelerating the groundwork, but don't use it as the whole nine yards until you have a solid set of prompts and can curate the outcome effectively.

Your core value prop often appears on homepage headlines and is a clear, succinct statement of the unique value you offer customers. This should be closely tied to your positioning and have one clear focal point. Length-wise, you're looking at around 10–15 words. Be careful when using Perplexity or ChatGPT because they often default to problem statements and hero headlines. You should try to use outcome-led messaging, as my experience has led me to understand that my prospect might not yet have identified their problem the way you have. In these cases, you will soon learn that prospects can immediately disengage from your online resource because they can't associate it with your problem statement. Outcome statements often tell people where they are headed and what transformation they buy, so always A/B test these things and then speak to your customers and prospects to double-check.

A good check to run when you finalize your positioning statements is to run them through ChatGPT or Perplexity and ask it to rewrite them for you at CEFR standard 16 years. Its The Common European Framework of Reference for Languages and it has standards from 11 to 25 years old. Sixteen is commonly used as an SEO target but test the statements at 16, 18, and 21 and see how they differ; a great way to get insights into simplicity of problem. In the US, the American Council on the Teaching of Foreign Languages (ACTFL) is the equivalent standard; I haven't tried the exercise with this before, but feel free to try.

12

Positioning Strategies in Competitive Markets

COMPETITIVE POSITIONING IS the process of defining how a brand or product differentiates itself from competitors in the minds of customers. Here, you aim to establish a unique value proposition and identity in the market. Your main goal is to create a distinct and favorable position in the target market's mind, giving customers a compelling reason to choose your brand, product, or service over your competitors. To achieve this, you need to master these four elements:

- Understanding your target audience
- Analyzing competitors
- Identifying your unique strengths and value proposition
- Crafting a clear positioning statement

These steps are important as effective positioning helps attract customers, increase sales, and build brand loyalty by clearly communicating your unique value. The good thing is that by now you should have already gathered this information, or now by using this book as a guide, know why I asked you to perform as much analysis and research as possible. One effort leads to another, or at least supports another, and you start to gather momentum in your primary and secondary objectives for your new GTM.

The other thing I'd like to make clear is that positioning isn't a one and done exercise and most certainly you can have multiple positioning statements, one for each persona if you like. For example, in today's world we are selling to decision-making teams or buying committees. Gartner published a report that said there are up to 15 members in a decision-making committee, hence my personal opinion on why 40% of B2B deals never close. Too many decision-makers can only lead to inertia surely?

Anyway, if there are say at least five decision-makers on average or even just five members of a decision-making committee, you have to be able to position your product or service to each one of them, based on what's important to them. I would assume that a lot of companies set up these secondary email domains and then simply send mass copies of the same message to all committee members who then talk to each other and realize that no effort was made and they feel spammed, damaging your brand reputation.

Creating a Positioning Statement

Positioning is a crucial element of a successful go-to-market strategy. The problem is it often remains static for far too long and often misaligns with your customer far faster than you first think. I find this especially true for early-stage firms where the product may be constantly developing, and less so for more mature firms firmly planted in their marketplaces. In reality, your positioning should mature with your audience's understanding of your product or service but also with the product's use case or the job (JTBD) that your product or service is hired to perform. I believe it should also be data-driven and segment-focused; that is, you don't have a single position to adopt, but rather you have multiple positions or positioning statements to the differing segments or personas in your customer and prospect audiences.

To effectively develop a positioning framework, I'm going to assume you've already defined your customer segment or persona. If not, we recommend first exploring our persona eBook and completing the exercises therein. Find this in the supporting portal listed in the back of the book.

- First, establish a review date. Before getting started, set a date to reassess the document you create, as your product, markets, or customer base may evolve over time. I like a quarterly review as it's long enough for you to learn from your audience if your positioning is working before pivoting, if needed.
- Subsequently, craft your product description. Keep it brief, including elements such as the name, key features, and issues you're addressing. Strive to contain it within one or two sentences.
- Then, outline your category; consider it an overview of your product marketplace. Delineate the market in which you compete and emphasize any distinguishing factors—e.g., unlike market X, our market is inherently anxious and financially constrained.
- After your category overview, depict the competition. If customers aren't purchasing from you, who are they turning to? List the top contenders here along with their weaknesses relative to your offering.
- Once you've completed the above, characterize your persona. If your personas differ significantly, you might want to create separate positioning documents for each. In this case, this is where you describe the persona in question.

To finalize the framework, define three additional pieces of information. Create a spreadsheet (if you haven't already) with three columns. Label them as follows: unique differentiator, the challenge, and the value. Then address the following questions:

- **Unique Differentiator:** What aspect of your product sets you apart from competitors? The focus here is on uniqueness; if your competitor offers the same feature, it doesn't belong in this section.
- **The Challenge:** What issue(s) are your customers facing due to the absence of this feature?
- **The Value:** How does your unique attribute resolve that challenge? Draw upon emotion, utopian visions, and real-life testimonials where possible.

List as many unique features as you can, then address the challenge and value questions. By doing this periodically, you'll always be able to position your product or service effectively for its target market or audience. There are six key components to drafting your positioning statement, but remember that your business may have a need for more than one position statement!

- **Competitive Alternatives**—what customers would do if your solution didn't exist
- **Unique Attributes**—the features and capabilities that you have that alternatives lack
- **Value and Proof**—the benefits that those features enable for customers and case studies or testimonials
- **Target Market Characteristics**—the characteristics of a group of buyers that really care a lot about the value you deliver
- **Market Category**—the market you describe yourself as being part of so that customers understand your value proposition
- **Relevant Trends**—trends that your customers understand and/or are interested in that can help make your product more relevant right now

With all this now completed, you need to develop a storytelling strategy like I mentioned earlier in this book. Either revert back to those, or another commonly used option is Freytag's Pyramid, which has five stages to its story:

1. **Beginning:** This is where we meet the characters and learn about where the story takes place. It's like the introduction to a book.
2. **Building Tension:** Things start to get more exciting here. Problems appear, and the main character faces challenges. It's like climbing up a hill—things get harder as you go.
3. **Most Exciting Part:** This is the top of the pyramid. It's the most thrilling part of the story, where the biggest problem happens. The main character has to make a big decision or face their biggest fear.

4. **Calming Down:** After the most exciting part, things start to settle. We see what happens because of the big event. It's like going down the other side of the hill.
5. **Ending:** This is where the story wraps up. We find out how everything turns out for the characters. It's like the last chapter of a book.

The original wording for Freytag's Pyramid differs from the above but the gist of the storytelling framework remains the same, maybe a little easier to understand. Using something like this to practice will help. If you use the frameworks from earlier in the book, upload those to an AI assistant and ask it with the pain points of your persona(s) or a full persona profile to create a landing page in a table format. You can get some pretty cool results to help fire up your marketing and sales campaigns. Once you do that, go back to my CEFR challenge and test different language levels to see how simplified your product or service offering could be communicated.

13

Aligning Sales and Marketing Goals

Creating a Unified Customer Journey

In this chapter, we look at the key success factor of a well-executed GTM strategy, sales and marketing alignment. The thing I don't like about this is that we have been calling for it since the turn of the century alongside personalization at scale, and yet, time and again, companies allow these two departments to go to war with each other. More commonly than not, marketing has to fight harder than other teams to prove its value in the C-Suite/Boardroom, and even when it does, the ways it does are still called into question. So if the C-Suite can't enforce change and strategic alignment, then make sure you rehire people who will. In Gartner's 2023 State of Go To Market Report, they stated that 70% of GTM strategies fail because of a lack of alignment in marketing and sales. Just sit and digest that and think about why you now might want to execute each step covered in this book and the ARISE framework.

The easiest way to start to align marketing and sales strategy is with a workshop: both teams, in a room completely aligned on how they are going to bring new business. They need data, the voice of the customer feedback, and a lot of the research we suggested earlier in this book, and each other's experience, and it should play out something like this.

Workshop Objectives

1. Foster better understanding between marketing and sales teams
2. Align goals and strategies
3. Improve communication and collaboration
4. Enhance lead quality and conversion rates
5. Develop a unified customer journey approach

Pre-Workshop Preparation

Gather Data

- Analyze current sales and marketing metrics.
- Collect feedback from both teams on past and present performance, including wins losses and passed-over tactics and opportunities.
- Review customer feedback and any previous journey maps.

Set Clear Goals

- Define specific, measurable outcomes for the workshop. You want to make sure that when you align marketing and sales, marketing is running a campaign, and sales is running a complementary sales campaign with the same messaging.
- Identify key pain points to address. Remember, you are not trying to reinforce current beliefs; you are trying to establish the facts and nothing more. Anything else carries bias and you want to move as far from that mindset as possible.

Choose Participants

- Include key stakeholders from both departments, but if possible, don't let leaders run the sessions, often, leaders have their own ideas of what good looks like that can blur the outcome.

Workshop Structure

Opening Session

- **Ice-breaker Activity**: Start with a team-building exercise to foster camaraderie. It should be fun and lighthearted and, if possible, unrelated to the workshop's goal.
- **Overview Presentation**: Explain workshop goals and agenda.

Understanding Each Other

- **Role Swap Exercise**: Have marketing and sales team members describe each other's roles and use as much detail as possible. Document any and all assumptions and use sticky notes to create internal sales and marketing personas.
- **Pain Point Sharing**: Discuss challenges faced by each team.

Aligning Goals and Metrics

- **Goal-Setting Activity**: Collaboratively define shared objectives and how each team can support those activities. Have each team tell the other what good would look like.
- **KPI Alignment**: Agree on key performance indicators that matter to both teams.

Lead Management Process

- **Lead Scoring Workshop**: Develop a shared understanding of lead quality. Personally, I am not a fan of marketing qualified leads (MQLs); for me, they are for marketing to show that marketing works but they don't contribute directly to revenue. Agree on the sales-qualified lead (SQL) and work towards what a marketing-generated/sales-qualified lead looks like.
- **Lead Handoff Protocol**: Create a clear process for transferring leads from marketing to sales. This is true but also insinuates

there is a handoff; in fact, the best alignment uses different forms of marketing across the customer lifecycle. So when the prospect becomes an SQL what you want to have marketing do is ensure case studies, decks, and materials are ready for the next part of the journey, but to stay aligned.

Content Collaboration

- **Content Audit**: Review existing marketing materials and sales collateral. Look at what's been working and what hasn't and look for feedback on why.
- **Content Creation Brainstorm:** Identify gaps and plan new content that serves both teams based on your new research.

Customer Journey Mapping

- **Journey Mapping Exercise**: Collaboratively map the customer journey from awareness to advocate.
- **Touchpoint Analysis**: Identify key interactions and responsibilities for each team.

Action Planning

- **SMART Goal Setting**: Develop specific, measurable, achievable, relevant, and time-bound goals.
- **Task Assignment:** Clearly define responsibilities and next steps.

Post-Workshop Follow-up

Documentation

- Summarize workshop outcomes and action items
- Distribute to all participants and relevant stakeholders

Implementation Plan

- Create a timeline for implementing agreed-upon changes
- Assign owners to each action item

Regular Check-ins

- Schedule follow-up meetings to track progress
- Address any challenges in the implementation

Measure Results

- Track key metrics to evaluate the impact of alignment efforts
- Celebrate successes and address shortcomings

Interestingly enough, many of the activities mentioned in this example alignment workshop already form part of the wider ARISE approach; however, sometimes you really need to bring the organization on the journey with you rather than operate in a silo on your own and then relay your findings to an unappreciative or unreceptive audience. Bookmark this approach and revert once you finish reading this book.

Customer Journey Mapping

Earlier in this book, we touched on mapping the customer journey. In this section, we want to focus on funnel stages and tactics. That is what each team can do across each stage of the journey. Consider that there are five commonly accepted buyer journey stages: awareness, interest, consideration, decision-making, and relationship. This covers the journey from stranger to promoter for the customers or segments that you work with. Note, while there may be overlap between customer journeys for segments, noting the nuances, if any, for each can be a fruitful endeavor to understand.

Awareness   This stage of the journey focuses on new business opportunities. It wants to draw potential customers into your messaging channels in order to build brand awareness. Your aim here is to keep them becoming more aware of your brand, product, or service.

Interest   Now that you have somebody's attention, you want to spend time nurturing that budding relationship with content, webinars, social media, and other content marketing tactics. Your aim here is to capture their details and deepen the relationship.

Consideration At this stage you are aiming to help the prospect rationalize if this product or service is right for them. Think about the multiple ways you can aid this process including content, landing pages, blogs, self-serve demos, product demos, chatbots, case studies, and more.

Decision-making Now that the prospect has decided to evaluate your product and is considering you as the solution provider, you have to walk them through the finish line. Align to the customer's outcomes, ensuring that you focus on helping them achieve their goals and close the deal.

Relationship Now that you've closed the deal, how is the client handed off, onboarded, made safe, and provided quick time to value? Your customer success team is involved here, but the onboarding should be as automated as possible upon notification of a closed-won deal. With today's automation tools and integrated customer platforms like HubSpot, this should be a seamless process triggered automatically time and time again. You can then measure your performance digitally and work on enhancing the onboarding process over time.

Based on the research and the results of this workshop, what you have to collectively decide are the steps each team takes for outbound and inbound activities to ensure that your messaging is aligned with the goals and KPIs for each given stage of the funnel. Use the simple approach below to align activities and approaches between teams.

Marketing Opportunities

- Awareness
- Interest
- Consideration
- Decision-making
- Relationship

Sales Opportunities

- Awareness
- Interest

- Consideration
- Decision-making
- Relationship

Customer Success Opportunities

- Relationship

Answer the stages listed above and you can easily see where the teams align or misalign and you can course correct. Once you have alignment you need to focus on your sales enablement strategy. This is where marketing can work with sales to design and build assets that enable a smooth flow from SQL to paid customer.

Developing Sales Enablement Materials

Sales enablement is about designing your sales process, supporting documents, sales training, and your sales tech stack. It's about setting out to understand what works and what does not and being able to implement change because you can follow the data. Now, here's the thing: I have so many founders tell me that sales enablement isn't suitable for early-stage firms, and to be honest, I am tired of hearing it. If we keep telling those with the least experience that process and structure do not matter, we'll always go to market with a misguided notion that what matters doesn't. And founders, especially technical ones, will always look to their sales hires to solve the revenue problem and for that to happen you need some grade A sales reps, and many do not have the budget or understanding of how to hire one. Every time you set out with a sales approach, you need to be able to measure it so you can iterate, spot bottlenecks and optimize the sales and marketing lifecycle.

So how do you get started?

First, you need to break down your process. Analyze the sales cycle, understand who your customers are, and how many people are in the decision-making process. This gives you a solid understanding of where to begin. You also need to understand your competitive landscape, this also plays a key role in your enablement process. Let's break this down into stages.

Customer journey mapping: by now, you should have this done. Using your data from your CRM and marketing tools, you should have clearly identified the customer journey through your channels. Cover from stranger to advocate. If you have yet to define it, work cross functionally with your customer-facing teams to do so.

Customer experience mapping: start by collecting quantitative and qualitative information about your clients. Items you may consider are customer surveys, product usage information, demographic data, website analytics, personas, and software or service reviews. Consider how the customer engages with your organization, for example, how their identified problem led them to your solution, how they analyzed your value proposition and evaluated the competition, what the internal decision-making process looked like, and how they will use your product or service inside their company.

Put additional focus on the motivating factors and influences that drive your customers and prospects; think what are their needs and what are they thinking and doing to get their needs served? You also need to develop new KPIs to align with the sales enablement process so that you can effectively and efficiently measure your future performance.

Develop your enablement assets: in order to deliver a robust sales process, not only do you require a map of the sales process—that is a step-by-step playbook to qualifying, evaluating and landing the account, you will also need to create:

- Sales email sequences for each persona, product, and decision-maker
- Sales scripts for reps for outbound sales
- Objection handling scripts for situational objection handling and battle cards for competitive objection handling
- Product one-pagers that highlight features, benefits, and outcomes
- Cross-sell and upsell email sequences
- A product demo playbook for sales-led products
- A freemium to paid playbook for product-led companies
- A set of case study questions

The good thing about today's CRM tools like HubSpot is that you can create all of this and then install it into the CRM, track its performance and then iterate from there. Looking back at that list I'd likely add the win/loss interviews and automate the interview requests off of the back of each and every closed won or closed lost deal. Here are a few tips on what not to accept as success when it comes to sales rep reporting:

- The number of calls made, connected, voicemails left, etc.
- The number of emails sent
- The number of emails opened (although it is a good indicator that your email headlines work)

What you do want to care about are:

- The number of responses to emails and the content of those responses
- The number of meetings booked
- The number of demos booked
- The number of times a competitive battle card was used
- The number of times the objection handling playbook was used
- The conversion rate of your cross-sell and upsell sequences
- Your freemium to paid conversion rates
- The number of demos converted
- The win/loss ratio of deals
- Revenue

All of these will help you focus on what matters in the output from your sales enablement program. The final thing you want to add to this is a regular sales confidence survey. This should be a monthly survey with the sales team, much like an internal NPS (Net Promoter Score) survey you would use for your customer success and onboarding. If you do go all in on HubSpot after reading this book, you can set this survey up directly out of the service hub and track effectiveness there. Track the sentiment and specific feedback from the sales team and use this to help shape your enablement program over the longer term. Again, remember that you still need to correlate the feedback from the group, so that you ensure all reps either like or dislike the assets and look into individual points collectively for a wider perspective. In the next chapter, we discuss another sales favorite: pricing!

14

Pricing and Revenue Models

When it comes to pricing and revenue models, I have to admit it's my area with the least practiced expertise. However, there are three key elements you need to consider: the pricing model, the pricing strategy, and the pricing policy. Each is as important as the last and vitally important to your success. Let's start with pricing models.

Pricing Models

So, there are quite a few pricing models out there, and each has its own pros and cons. Let me walk you through some of the most common ones and give you my take on them:

Flat-rate Pricing

This is as simple as it gets. One product, one set of features, one price. It's straightforward, but it's not very flexible. You've got to make that offer really tempting because you only get one shot at winning over customers. There's always the discount, but you shouldn't go to market with discounts front of mind.

Usage-based Pricing

Think of this as pay-as-you-go. The more a customer uses your software, the higher their bill. It's fair, but it can make it hard for customers to predict their costs. This model has long been combined with flat rate pricing so that it makes it easy for customers to get a price they can easily understand and then a scaling charge for additional usage.

Tiered Pricing

This is where you offer different packages with different features. It's great because you can appeal to different types of customers, but it can sometimes confuse people in the sales funnel. Tiers are good, but often, you can run into situations where the next tier can be unaffordable or out of touch with the customer's needs. For example, let's say you fix access to a feature at a lower tier but the user needs more of that feature and not everything else involved, then they could end up looking for another product that's more flexible and that hurts your bottom line.

Per-seat Pricing

With this model, customers pay a fixed price per user. It's easy to understand, but some customers might try to cheat by sharing logins. The challenge for concurrent logins isn't as bad as you may think as you can you can design your software to prevent multiple logins at the same time. Software to guard against this is available in the market, but it is complex to navigate and mainly useful in enterprise software.

Per Active User Pricing

This is similar to per-seat pricing, but customers only pay for active users. It's great for big companies but not so much for smaller businesses.

Per-feature Pricing

Here, you price based on the features you offer. It can be a good way to encourage upgrades, but it's tricky to get the balance right. I think this strategy provides little value on its own, and the usage-based pricing model with a flat rate model can negate the need for this. However, if I sit back and think about this, you could potentially use this in a "build your own" format of software features, but I can't say that I have seen this used widely.

Per Result or Outcome Pricing

Many large firms offering AI agents are introducing outcome-based pricing. It's a great approach for a service provider that wants to offer value at scale but respect that people know AI is serving them. Outcome-based pricing for service agents makes sense, with fees as low as 99 cents for an outcome. This means the user only pays for results and can choose how to use the agents according to their needs rather than pay a subscription.

Customizable Pricing

This lets customers pick and choose the features they want. It's flexible, but it can make your revenue unpredictable. It also feels quite similar to feature-based pricing but is more commonly used in sales-led products that target the enterprise as well as the SMB or mid-market. When you look at the pricing page of software with customizable pricing, it's nearly always labeled as their enterprise offer.

Freemium Pricing

You offer a basic version for free and charge for premium features. It can get you lots of users, but not all of them will pay. The freemium pricing model is widely adopted by product-led companies. That is, those who expect their product to sell itself to users who experience its value before paying. More commonly referred to as the "open-top" model, it's a great way to get a lot of people to try your product without committing unless they find the value and success they seek.

Freemium with Ads Pricing

Like freemium, but you show ads to free users. It guarantees some income, but ads can annoy people. This model is widely used by gaming companies to enable your ongoing free experience, and many of them now use ads as a way to earn credits on the game, integrating premium in-game offers with supplementary ad-watching credits. Also now adopted by streaming platforms like Prime, Netflix and Spotify.

Pricing Strategies

Now, let's talk about pricing strategies. These are more about how you approach setting your prices:

Cost-plus Pricing

This is pretty straightforward. You add up your costs, tack on some profit, and there's your price. It's simple, but it doesn't take into account what customers are willing to pay. Experts often question this approach because it isn't based on research, and without talking to your prospective customers, you'll never know the true value of the product or service, potentially leaving money on the table.

Competitor-based Pricing

Here, you look at what your competitors are charging and base your prices on that. It's a good starting point, especially if you're new to the market. But, it is not foolproof. Just because there are incumbent players in your space does not mean that their pricing is your pricing. The nuances of your product could make the value proposition more worthy to the buyer, and again, you could leave money on the table if you aren't truly investigating and speaking to people.

Value-based Pricing

This strategy involves asking your customers what they expect and what they're willing to pay. It takes more time, but it can help you nail your market value. This is my favorite model. It allows you to stand out because of the value you provide, and it works effectively well for both product and service companies. In a service company, your value is in your earned experience, proprietary methodologies, and systems and in tech, it's your features, benefits, and niche focus. If you serve a huge pain point and it is underserved, your value is high, whereas an over-served market can see your value drop.

Market Penetration Pricing

With this approach, you set your prices low to break into the market quickly. It can help you gain customers fast, but it might not be sustainable in the long run. Discounting for long-term subscriptions can make sense, and you can always grandfather clients to an early-stage pricing model if you feel you may lose them as you increase your prices.

Premium Pricing

This takes the approach that higher subscription costs mean better quality. So you charge above the market value for your product, with the explanation your product offers more to your audience than your competitors. Remember if your product doesn't offer at least what the incumbents do, then this model will likely not work and could negatively impact revenues through poor online reviews and feedback.

Skimming

This is the opposite of the market penetration strategy. Here you make your subscription price high. The belief behind this is customer demand will decrease the longer your product is available. So, you can lower the subscription cost over time—which makes it increasingly competitive in the market.

Remember, there's no one-size-fits-all solution here. The best approach often involves a combination of these models and strategies tailored to your specific product and market. It's all about finding what works best for your business and your customers.

Building a Pricing Strategy Framework

I can't stress enough how important it is to have a solid pricing strategy framework in place. When I think about pricing, I see it as one of the most powerful tools we have in our go-to-market toolkit. It's not just about slapping a number on a product; pricing can make or break a company's success. First off, you need to understand that pricing isn't just about covering costs and making a profit. It's about positioning your product in the market, influencing customer perceptions, and achieving your business goals. Whether you're aiming to maximize revenue, gain market share, or establish yourself as a premium brand, your pricing strategy plays a pivotal role. Now, let me walk you through some key elements of a pricing strategy framework.

Understanding Your Objectives

Be crystal clear about what you're trying to achieve. Are you looking to increase sales volume? Boost profit margins? Penetrate a new market? Your pricing strategy should align with these goals. Yet, you can't price your products in a vacuum. You need to consider:

1. **Customer Demand:** How much are your target customers willing to pay?
2. **Competitive Landscape:** What are your competitors charging?
3. **Cost Structure:** What are your production and operational costs?

You can see by looking at the questions how some founders and business leaders try cost-plus and competitor-based pricing models. But the temptation to just jump in and run with your gut could be the thing that sinks your ship. The best approach is to create a pricing policy that governs how the business approaches this.

Setting Up a Pricing Policy

Once you've chosen your strategy, you need to implement it carefully and set up a pricing policy. Although I have touched on this subject last, it's the first thing that I would do. I covered models and strategies as it's easier for those least experienced with pricing to understand them and their application before painting a broader picture on how to manage the process. This is a comprehensive overview of what goes into a pricing strategy.

Setting up a pricing policy is a complex process that involves several key factors and steps. Based on the information provided, here's a comprehensive overview of what goes into establishing a pricing policy.

Determine Pricing Objectives

The first step is to set clear pricing objectives, which can include:

- Customer value-based objectives
- Cost-based objectives
- Sales-oriented objectives
- Market share-oriented objectives
- Target return objectives
- Competition-oriented objectives
- Customer-driven objectives

It's common for companies to have multiple objectives, as they guide the overall pricing strategy. Choose your objectives carefully.

Estimate Demand

Understanding market demand is crucial. This involves:

- Analyzing customer behavior and preferences
- Conducting market research
- Assessing price elasticity of demand
- Evaluating customer willingness to pay

Estimate Costs

A thorough cost analysis is essential, including:

- Fixed costs (e.g., rent, salaries)
- Variable costs (e.g., materials, production costs)
- Total cost of production or service delivery

Analyze the External Environment

Using a PESTLE analysis to consider external factors:

- Political factors
- Economic conditions
- Social trends
- Technological advancements
- Legal considerations
- Environmental factors

Select Pricing Strategies or Tactics

Choose appropriate pricing strategies based on your objectives and analysis. Common strategies include:

- Cost-plus pricing
- Value-based pricing
- Competition-based pricing
- Penetration pricing
- Skimming pricing

Consider Additional Factors

- **Competitor Pricing**: Analyze what similar products or services are priced at in the market
- **Value Proposition**: Identify your unique selling points that justify your pricing
- **Marketing Strategy**: Align pricing with overall marketing objectives and promotional activities
- **Profit Margins**: Ensure pricing allows for sustainable profit margins

Implement and Monitor

- Set up systems to implement the chosen pricing strategy
- Regularly review and adjust prices based on market conditions and performance
- Analyze the impact of pricing on sales, market share, and profitability

Legal and Ethical Considerations

- Ensure pricing practices comply with legal regulations
- Avoid unethical practices like price fixing or predatory pricing

Setting up a pricing policy is an ongoing process that requires regular review and adjustment. You have to balance profitability with customer perception of value, while remaining competitive in the market. The ultimate goal is to create a pricing strategy that maximizes profits while providing value to customers and achieving the company's overall objectives. The good thing here is that you should have covered this in the assessment stage of ARISE and all of the voice of the customer work in the research phase would have informed you on how well you are performing against the market. So now you understand pricing models and strategies and you have a pricing strategy framework from which to work. I guess we should look at how you can optimize pricing and revenue models.

Optimizing Revenue Models for SaaS and Fintech

When it comes to optimizing pricing models for SaaS and fintech products or service companies, there are a few key strategies I would recommend:

Use Value-based Pricing

Focus on the value your product or service provides to customers rather than just costs. Understand what specific pain points you're solving and how much that's worth to different customer segments. This allows you to price based on the value delivered rather than arbitrary tiers or undervalued expertise.

Implement Usage-based Pricing

For many SaaS and fintech products, usage-based pricing aligns well with the value provided. Charge based on key usage metrics like number of transactions, API calls, storage used, etc. This allows you to capture more revenue from power users while keeping costs low for smaller customers.

Offer Tiered Pricing Plans

Create three to four pricing tiers targeted at different customer segments. For example, a basic tier for small businesses, a professional tier for mid-market, and an enterprise tier for large customers. This allows you to capture more value from larger customers willing to pay more.

Use Per-user Pricing Strategically

Per-user pricing can work well for collaboration and team-based tools. However, be careful not to disincentivize adding users. Consider offering volume discounts or only charging for active users.

Leverage Freemium Models

Offering a free tier with limited functionality can be a great way to acquire users and drive adoption. Then upsell those users to paid plans over time as they get value from the product.

Experiment with Pricing

Don't be afraid to test different pricing models and price points. Use segmented testing to optimize your pricing over time based on conversion rates and customer feedback.

Consider Bundling

Package complementary features or products together at a discount. This can increase average contract value and provide more value to customers.

Use Dynamic Pricing

Especially for fintech products, consider using algorithms to dynamically adjust pricing based on market conditions, risk profiles, etc.

Offer Annual Contracts

Incentivize customers to pay annually by offering a discount compared to monthly pricing. This improves cash flow and reduces churn.

Analyze Unit Economics

Closely track key metrics like customer acquisition cost (CAC), lifetime value (LTV), churn, etc. Use this data to optimize your pricing and ensure you have a sustainable business model.

Provide Transparent Pricing

Make your pricing easy to understand. Hidden fees or complex pricing structures can turn off potential customers.

The key is to align your pricing with the value you provide, while also considering your costs, competitive landscape, and target customers. Regularly review and optimize your pricing strategy as your product and market evolves.

PART

VII

Execute

"Quality is never an accident; it is always the result of high intention, sincere effort, intelligent direction and skillful execution; it represents the wise choice of many alternatives."

—William A. Foster

15

Creating a Comprehensive GTM Plan

Integrating Insights from Previous Stages

This entire book is about developing a comprehensive go-to-market plan. It's about best practice, internal team alignment, technology, and a repeatable process that drives your flywheel as you grow. So, in this chapter I want to break down how I would plan it based on the work we did to shift my agency in summer 2023. The first thing I can remember was using a spreadsheet, and why not? They are a welcome asset for any sales or marketing expert worth their salt. Now, if you can, cast your mind back to earlier in this book. I told you that I used a service design workshop to begin the process, but before that I had also done my customer and persona research.

I want you to remember that so that you can follow me to your own success. After the workshop, we created productized versions of our services that were comprehensive and spoke to the different personas we typically engaged with. Once I had those products fleshed out, I created my RevOps Alignment Campaign Planning worksheet, and it looked like this:

Strategy and Planning

- Row 1: Annual Brand Campaign Theme (Heroes)
- Row 2: A cell (×5) for each product we created with links to each product messaging framework
- Row 3: A link to the service design workshop workbook with research and outcomes
- Row 4: Each cell in the row is linked to a buyer journey map completed on a Miro board, one per product
- Row 5: Each cell is linked to the main persona for each product
- Row 6: Each cell is linked to an individual "buyer funnel stages and tactics plan" for each product
- Row 7: A content mapping framework for each product per cell
- Row 8: A segment hypothesis set for each product
- Row 9: A segment audit for each product
- Row 10: A launch checklist for each product

Marketing Campaign Strategy

- Row 11: The theme for each product's marketing strategy
- Row 12: Types of memes acceptable for each product marketing strategy
- Row 13: A list of blog posts for each product in cells
- Row 14: A link to custom-built GTM assessments for each product
- Row 15: Links to articles on Entrepreneur.com for each product
- Row 16: Links to articles for Medium.com
- Row 17: Go to market checklist for each product
- Row 18: A link to the ebook for each product
- Row 19: The webinar plan for each product
- Row 20: Links to the landing pages for each product
- Row 21: Links to meetups and events for each product
- Row 22: Links to case studies for each product
- Row 23: Links to online testimonials for each product underlying services
- Row 24: Links to videos for each product
- Row 25: Links to your Service Design Workshop Book

- Row 26: Links to the paid adverts for each product
- Row 27: The podcast episode for each underlying service per product

Sales Preparation

- Row 28: Intent keywords for each product for use in Rollworks
- Row 29: Links to battle cards for each product
- Row 30: Links to objection handling scripts for each product
- Row 31: Links to sales email templates for each product
- Row 32: Links to sales one-pagers for each product
- Row 33: Links to sales calling scripts for each product
- Row 34: Links to cross-sell email sequences for each product
- Row 35: Links to upsell emails for each product
- Row 36: Links to funnel stages and tactics for each product

Customer Onboarding

- Row 37: Onboarding playbooks for each product linked to cells
- Row 38: Customer journey map for each product
- Row 39: Health scoring for each onboarding plan per product

Sales Products and Delivery Planning

- Row 40: Kick-off workshop playbook per product
- Row 41: The ARISE strategy for each product
- Row 42: Service delivery KPIs for each product

Account Expansion

- Row 43: Upsell playbook for each product
- Row 44: Cross-sell playbook for each product

Now you may be thinking, why on earth did I list those bullet points?

The reason is that it shows what goes into planning to launch a product and why, even when you have untested products for the market, you should plan everything from start to finish. What that plan enabled me to do was have a manual blueprint to revenue operations that I could replicate into HubSpot and repeat for my clients. Note this is the level of detail we get into when we deliver our services. I can't even count how many assets and swipe files were used and created in order to build the sub-materials that linked to this master spreadsheet, but I can tell you there were five products created from the service design workshop. It's also available in the resources site linked at the back of this book.

One product was for marketing, one for sales, one for customer success, one for product teams and then we have our web product for apps and websites. They are all really comprehensive solutions with a choice of tactics. For example, the marketing product covers most things today's CMO or growth lead needs help with. Tactically, that product is supported by PLG, ABM, or Demand Generation, but how can you sell a tactic to someone who may not yet have identified their problem? I think this is why agency websites often fail to deliver and why they don't focus on their own marketing and lead generation.

A year later, now November 2024, while writing this, I revisited our GTM, reapplied ARISE, and accessed more data, and we learned something new. We paid more attention to our first-party data than last time around when we lent into our third-party data and research more. This time, we identified four key customer segments in the work we do based on the type of enquiries and business we close.

- **Segment One 60%:** SaaS, fintech and management consulting firms needing optimized GTM strategic support.
- **Segment Two 20%:** SaaS, fintech and management consulting firms needing a revenue operations service
- **Segment Three 10%:** Tech firms needing ABM services
- **Segment Four 10%:** Enterprise tech firms spinning out a new product and launching a startup

That's it. It's not defined by tactical support; it's now defined by the problems we are asked to solve, and this has fed into the updated website and the way we present ourselves to the market. The value proposition is clear, and how we help is defined and based on past results. We have metrics tied into our outcomes so that you can ask, "What results would we expect if we work together?"

This isn't a plug. I want you to understand that I started by answering the questions: how do you plan to convey your value; enable your buyer to buy from you; and plan to onboard, retain, upsell, and cross-sell your customer base? This is the answer to the questions I posed much earlier in this book. In fact, bar the execution of each campaign, you are seeing the outcome of all the hard work that ARISE asks of you come to fruition. Now, with the rise of AI and large language models, you can use all of the data you would create with this methodology to amplify what you should produce, for which customer segments at speed and scale, giving you a competitive advantage. IF you adopt it.

A Go-to-market Strategy Planner

We've honestly covered a lot of ground so far, but there are more things you need to have in place beyond what's already been discussed. Let's first look at where you should start for planning your product launch.

1. Define your audience: personas, decision-makers, ideal customer profile (ICP)
2. Describe the outcomes and how your product benefits each of the above
3. Define your primary and secondary objectives for this campaign
4. Describe the pain points of each persona and how your product solves that pain
5. Describe the value your clients get from your research for the product
6. Create messaging frameworks for your product for each audience type
7. Collect the evidence in testimonials and case studies that support your claims
8. Define the buyer journey for each persona and build lead-scoring calculations for marketing qualified leads (MQLs) and sales-qualified leads (SQLs)
9. Define your pricing policy and strategy
10. Build your marketing and sales plan for the year

11. Define the key performance indicators for measuring how the campaigns perform
12. Execute, measure, and experiment

Collectively, this chapter has provided you with a lot of solid direction and guidance around GTM strategic planning, but to cap it all off, we need one last thing: a product launch checklist.

Product Launch Checklist

A product launch checklist can be executed in several ways. Two preferred approaches are a shared spreadsheet or Google Doc or a project management tool. This checklist has to confirm that this go-to-market strategy has been successfully assessed, researched, created, strategically applied, and is ready to be executed.

Market Analysis

- Did you define the purpose of your analysis?
- Do you know the size of the available market?
- Have you effectively researched and analyzed the competition?
- Have you acted on your findings?

Persona Research

- Did you define what you wanted to learn?
- Did you talk to your personas through interviews, surveys, and feedback loops?
- Did you run internal persona workshops to learn what teams and individuals know about them?
- Was your research both qualitative and quantitative?
- Are any hypothetical ideas removed from your personas?

Pricing

- Is your pricing based on the goals of your business?
- Did you perform a competitive pricing analysis?

- Did you run value-based pricing interviews with customers and prospects?
- Did you build a pricing policy to govern your pricing strategy?
- Did you decide on offers for new and current customers?

Positioning

- Do you now understand which problems you solve for your customers?
- Do you know what job customers hire your product or service to solve?
- Have you updated your positioning statements?
- Defined a clearer value proposition?
- Built a strong and tested storytelling framework?

Goals

- Do you now have SMART goals for each product or service strategy?
- Are your team goals directly aligned to the overall business strategy?
- Do individual contributors know what part they play in achieving the goals and objectives?

GTM Launch

- Does your new positioning reflect on marketing and sales assets, including your website?
- Is your marketing plan signed off?
- Your sales strategy?
- Your onboarding plan?
- Is your tech stack properly aligned and implemented?
- Are your enablement materials signed off and are the reps trained to use them?
- Is your voice of the customer plan fully ingrained in your new GTM plan?
- Are all your marketing materials created and signed off?

- Do you have a comms plan for the launch?
- Do you now have a cross-functional team for moving forward in alignment?
- Do you have a list of pre-planned experiments incase things don't go to plan?
- A crisis management plan?
- Well-documented feedback loops?

All of the above will help you understand where you are in terms of readiness for your new GTM launch. Of course, you can read this and point out things I didn't mention, and that's great. It means you're bought in, and you've engaged with the process, which is what I want the outcome to be. Each GTM plan should be unique to your business, even if you are following a guided playbook. It's the collective compound approach to growth, which is why ARISE is the perfect foil for the flywheel you've now set in motion for your product service or organization. For more support, tactics and swipe files, visit the website listed in the back of this book.

16

Resource Allocation and Budgeting

Identifying Required Resources

As part of the Assess stage of ARISE, we ask you to take stock of the team's skills and abilities; the reason for that is to help understand if you have the right people in place, because people are what help you win at go-to-market. Strategy is the roadmap, and tech is an enabler, but your biggest asset is the people going along for the ride. This is why you have to be ruthless when you are at work. You cannot carry passengers, dissenters, those who lack ability, who are there because they were there in the beginning. What matters is what works with people today, in this moment, in this time, for this stage of your journey. What strikes me as I write this, looking at my notes for the section that reads "identifying required resources," is the age-old problem of sacking the marketing team when the market moves against you. Personally, in times of need I would remove underperforming staff across the board first, then nice to have roles (and marketing isn't one of them—unless, of course, they are not performing), and then see where you stand. But to simply cut marketing as a budget line when the going gets tough is short-sighted, and short-termism rarely wins the war.

A Bain & Company article titled The New Recession Playbook expertly dives into how companies behave during recessions going back as far as the 1990–91 Savings and Loan Recession and coming back up to date with the COVID-19 recession. Their report shows that 47% of new rising star businesses are created during turbulent times rather than in stable times, but a whopping 89% of sinking ships are created in the same period. So, only a small number of companies know what moves to make. Bain goes on to say that there are three types of companies in a recession. Some that take a burn-the-furniture approach. Assuming that aggressive, across-the-board cost-cutting would get them through the downturn, they slash R&D budgets, for example, or they cut spending on sales and marketing activities that were key to growth, or they let go of valuable talent and ruled out acquisitions. Other companies made a misguided "try everything" move, straying from the company's core by betting on everything in a desperate bid for growth. And some companies simply waited too long before acting, so they were late to the party. Make the wrong decision or become indecisive, and it's already too late. You just might not yet know it.

What do winning companies do to prepare for recessions and downturns? Again, Bain looked at what has worked in the past. Those companies surgically restructure costs before the downturn, trimming the fat and preserving the muscle. They put their financial house in order, diligently managing liquidity and the balance sheet. They play offense by selectively reinvesting for competitive outperformance. And in a key move that enables them to emerge stronger than competitors, they aggressively pursue M&A opportunities. What you see here is that there's no panic or retrospective reaction that's already too late; they didn't simply cut the very tools that create growth. No, they were fiscally and operationally responsible, and that's why your team are your best asset. Cool heads prevail.

So, people are the number one resource you have to identify at all stages. Additionally, in the Assess stage, as well as assessing your talent you would have identified any issues in your tech stack, your processes and your current strategic implementation. These would be bookmarked for solution processing at this point in the methodology.

During the Research phase, which leans into further understanding your own competitive landscape, you would have learned even more about what other opportunities present that you could potentially take advantage of.

This would have been fully fleshed out in the Ideate stage, and now you should be looking at which of those are actually making it into your new forward strategy. As each business will come to its own understanding of its current situation, I'll give you some guidance on how you may distribute your budget, but take into consideration the stage and size of your business when doing so.

Budgeting Strategy for GTM

Staffing: 30–40% of Budget

As I previously mentioned, your team is critical for executing the go-to-market strategy successfully. This portion of the budget typically covers:

- Sales team salaries and commissions
- Marketing team salaries
- Customer support staff
- Product specialists

Technology: 15–25% of Budget

Technology enables and supports your go-to-market efforts. This allocation usually includes:

- CRM and sales automation tools
- Marketing automation platforms
- Analytics and reporting software
- Product demo/trial infrastructure
- Website and e-commerce platforms

The right tech stack can significantly boost efficiency and provide valuable insights. As a note to the reader, HubSpot can facilitate four out of the five things listed above and easily integrates with leading ecommerce platforms.

Customer Acquisition Channels: 35–50% of Budget

This is often the largest portion of the budget, covering various marketing and sales activities:

- Digital advertising (search, social, display)
- Content marketing and SEO
- Events and trade shows
- Public relations
- Direct mail campaigns (ABM specific)
- Partner/channel marketing

The specific allocation within this category will depend on your target audience and which channels are most effective for reaching them, which, of course, you would have established way back in the process and will now be ready to execute. It's important to note that these percentages can vary based on factors like:

- Company size and stage
- Industry and competitive landscape
- Product complexity
- Target market characteristics
- Sales cycle length

Additional Considerations

- **Market Research:** Allocate 5–10% for ongoing market research to stay informed about customer needs and competitive landscape.
- **Product Marketing:** Set aside 10–15% for developing messaging, sales enablement materials, and product launch activities.
- **Customer Retention:** Dedicate 10–15% to nurturing existing customers and driving upsells/cross-sells.

It's a difficult way to discuss this area of go-to-market strategy as it heavily relies on averages, which are still great guides; but for those seeking something more concrete, all I can offer is that you take your own circumstances into consideration and then go from there. Even today, as I write this book, I was looking at how I could build a performance calculator for my website at arisegtm.com that enables you to answer a few questions and take industry averages as a benchmark so that you could easily understand your own performance. What I discovered is that it's a complex process, even with the averages available to you.

B2B SaaS and fintech, for example, heavily overlap with their averages, with a lot of publicly available data showing a big unaccounted-for gap. For example, a lot of reports showed platforms with an ACV—Annual Contract Value of under $12k and then again at the top of over $250k, so what about platforms in the middle then? That's a huge space to understand, and let me share the areas I focused on understanding:

- Annual Contract Value (ACV)
- Annual Recurring Revenue (ARR)
- Top Quartile Net Retention Rate (NRR)
- Average Revenue Per Account (ARPA) under $500 p/m with NRR >100%
- Average Cost of Acquiring a Customer (CAC) by industry (SaaS, fintech, professional services)
- Which companies outperformed the median NRR of 100% and which did not
- What % of companies achieved an Annual Growth Rate of above 100% NRR
- What % of companies achieved Gross Revenue Retention (GRR) with the accepted industry standard? Minimum 90%
- What was the average industry churn rate
- What churn rate is actually deemed acceptable

All of this provides enough information for me to be able to calculate the anticipated performance improvement based on industry averages and your company's previous performance history. When you start building a new go-to-market strategy, it's not just about marketing, sales, customer success and ops, it's about economics, financial modeling and keeping your eyes firmly on the horizon. I mean imagine having a company that is operating at a 10% improvement year on year (YoY) and thinking it's doing well when the industry is operating at 20% or 25%? Yes it's good for you to see a 10% YoY revenue growth, but if you are underperforming drastically against the industry average and potentially your competitors, again it's something you need to understand, benchmark, and transform.

17

Setting KPIs and Success Metrics

Defining Success Metrics for GTM

In go-to-market there are typically two sets of metrics that govern and align the go-to-market across the organization; they are OKRs and KPIs.

OKRs

Objectives and Key Results (OKRs).

- **Objectives:** These are the aspirational goals that define what you want to achieve and should be short, inspirational, and engaging.
- **Key Results:** These are the specific, measurable outcomes that indicate progress towards achieving the objective. For each objective, you should have a set of two to five key results.

OKRs are set to keep people and teams engaged and aligned with larger organizational goals and strategies and provide employees with precise, comprehensive layouts of company goals and the plan to achieve them. They also ensure that all members of an organization are working toward a common direction at a constant pace with clear priorities. One of my favorite OKR tools with freemium access is Cascade: it is so simple to set your OKRs, attach KPIs, which I'll get to next, and track each team's performance to achieve the KPIs.

The visual tracking of how near to 100% of each KPI and in turn OKR is a great way to get all teams bought in, in a slightly gamified way. If you don't have a lot of experience with OKRs at your company, here are some tips to follow:

- Use clear, concise language that can be easily understood across the company
- Use verbs and clearly define the work to be done
- Set a deadline for each objective
- Make objectives ambitious yet realistic
- Constrain objectives to key priorities

To broaden your own understanding of metrics I suggest you read two books, if you haven't already done so:

1. Measure what matters by John Doerr for OKRs
2. KPI Checklists by Bernie Smith for 50 KPI checklist templates

I also have KPIs in the resources support site for the book you can access for free.

KPIs

Key Performance Indicators (KPIs)

- A quantifiable metric that measures how effectively an organization is achieving its goals

The purpose of KPIs is to help businesses evaluate the success of their activities, initiatives, or processes. They provide targets, milestones, and insights to help teams make better decisions. They can be used in many areas of a business, including finance, HR, marketing, and sales. For example, social media KPIs can measure the effectiveness of social media efforts and assess customer sentiment. The choice of KPIs is important because they must be designed to tell you a story of what is going on within the business at any given point in time. Far too often, KPIs end up being numbers in a report on a dashboard designed to support a narrative when they should, in fact, be designed to tell the truth, plain and simple.

As part of the ARISE GTM Methodology®, we kick off with around a 151 metrics across marketing, sales, customer success, people, and finance. Remember, if people are your best asset, then tracking how they feel within the organization isn't a nice to have but a must have and you can utilize HubSpot's Service Hub to build surveys that track employee sentiment, and you should also correlate how the workforce feels to the performance indicators in the funnel and ops. Unhappy talent equals unhappy teams, customers, and bottom line, high churn, toxic working environment, and so on. Also, this should be something only the HR or C-Suite look at. Team leaders should not have access unless the feedback is directly about their performance, and whistleblowing shitty behavior should be normalized, not pillorized to avoid long-term sickness absence and to just become an all-around decent place to work.

Marketing KPIs and Metrics

KPI	Metric	How you get there
MQL	Based on Lead Score	The cumulative pre-defined scoring of engagement points across your channels when a certain number is met e.g., 100.
Paid Ads	Spend to Conversions	The number of conversions from your ad spend as a %
	Impressions	The total number of served impressions from your ads
	Target Accounts Reached	The number of pre-defined target companies that engage with your ads
	Target Contacts Reached	The number of defined target contacts engaged by your ads at target companies
	Traffic Generated from Ads	The amount of individual visitors to a webpage from your ad spend

(*continued*)

(*continued*)

KPI	Metric	How you get there
	Click Through Rate	The number of clicks through your ads as a percentage
	Leads Generated	The total number of marketing-generated leads from your ad spend is typically confirmed as engaged in a buying cycle.
	Deals Generated	The total number of deals generated by your ad spend
	Deals Won	The total number of deals won per ad campaign
	Deals Lost	The total number of deals lost per ad campaign
	Cost Per Lead	The total cost of acquiring a lead by dividing ad spend by number of leads generated
Website Visitors	Visitors per Day	The number of individual visitors to the website daily
	Visitors per Week	The number of individual visitors to the website weekly
	Visitors per Month	The number of individual visitors to the website monthly
	Visitor Source	Where the visitors come from, e.g., direct search, referral, paid ads
Website Pages	Highest Conversion Pages	The pages on your site that have the most conversion activity
	Highest Conversions Forms Per Page	The highest converting forms by page
	Highest Pages for Dwell Time	Pages where visitors spend the longest time
	Highest Pages for Returning Visitors	The number of pages on your website that gets the most traffic regularly

KPI	Metric	How you get there
	Highest Pages for New Visitors	Pages with the highest volume of new visitors
	Total Number of Page Visits	The total number of page visits per journey by a visitor
	Top Pages	Top cumulative pages
	Top Blog Pages	Best performing blog content
	Average Time On Site	The total time of all website visitors on your site / by the number of visitors
Traffic	% of Traffic Booking Meetings	The number of meetings per month / by the number of website visitors
Best Performing Channels	Referral Traffic	Best channels referring traffic that converts
Social Media	Growth Per Channel	Month on month follower growth
	Referral Traffic	Traffic referred by channel
	Clicks Per Post by Campaign	Measure how many clicks each post gets at a campaign level
	Mentions Per Month	Measure how many times your brand is mentioned on your social channels each month
	Mentions Per Campaign	Measure how many times your brand is mentioned on your social channels each campaign
	Shares Per Month	The number of times your social posts are shared each month
	Shares Per Campaign	The number of times your social posts are shared per campaign

(continued)

(*continued*)

KPI	Metric	How you get there
	Retweets	How many times your tweets are retweeted on X (Twitter)
	Engagement— Comments Per Month	The total number of comments on your posts per month / by total number of followers per channel per month × 100
	Engagement— Comments Per Campaign	The total number of comments on your posts per month / by total number of followers per channel per campaign × 100
Email	Email Clickthrough Rate Per Campaign	The total number of unique clicks / number of delivered emails × 100
	Email Conversion Rate	Calculate your email conversion rate Email Conversion Rate = (Number of Conversions / Number of Delivered Emails) × 100
	Email Bounce Rate	Calculate your email bounce rate by measuring the number of bounced emails / number of delivered emails × 100
	Open Rate	Calculate your email bounce rate by measuring the number of opened emails / number of delivered emails × 100
	List Growth Rate	Calculate the number of new email addresses on your email list per month. The (Number of new subscribers—Number of unsubscribes) / Total number of email addresses on your list × 100

KPI	Metric	How you get there
	Unsubscribe Rate	Calculate the unsubscribe rate for your email campaigns.Unsubscribe Rate = (Number of Unsubscribes / Number of Delivered Emails) × 100
	Email Share/Forward Rate	Add a share or forward button to the email
	Overall ROI	Amount invested in campaign = Amount generated in sales—campaign cost × 100
	% of Unengaged Subscribers	To calculate the % of unengaged subscribers for your email list, it's the % of Unengaged Recipients = (Number of Unengaged Recipients / Total Number of Recipients) × 100
	New or Total Leads Generated	To track New Leads Generated = Number of new leads added to your database in a given time period
	Lead to Customer Conversion Rate	CTAs clicked that lead to paying customers
	Reply Rate	Calculate your email reply rate by measuring the number of sent emails / number of opened emails × 100

Remember these are a place to jump off from; these aren't your comprehensive list and, for example, the paid ads metrics, you would use these for each paid channel, LinkedIn Ads, Display, PPC, and any ABM Campaigns using tools like RollWorks. Next let's look at some sales metrics to kick off with.

Sales KPIs and Metrics

KPI	Metric	How you get there
SQL	Additional lead scoring or self-opted sales activities like booking a sales meeting or demo	Add points for sales meetings, product demos to lead scoring method
Sales Activities	Calls Made Per Day, Week, Month—Per Rep, Sales Team	Use connected services to your CRM like HubSpot's native calling features or platforms like Kixie or Aloware. They have associated performance reporting you can track.
	Average Call Pickup Time Per Rep, Sales Team	Track inbound sales calls by reps and the time to answer
	Emails Sent Per Day, Week, Month—Per Rep, SalesTeam	Track email performance from your CRM like HubSpot or Salesforce.
	Average Email Response Times Per Rep, Per Team	Track emails by rep and average time to respond
	Leads Worked Per Month	Track the number of worked leads monthly by rep and team through your CRM.
	Meetings Booked Per Day, Week, Month—Per Rep, Sales Team	Track this by rep meeting link, provided by the CRM or calendar software.
	LinkedIn Connections Made Per Day, Week, Month—Per Rep, Sales Team	Use tools like LinkedIn Sales Navigator and integrate that with HubSpot or use Hublead, a freemium option for the same.

KPI	Metric	How you get there
	LinkedIn InMails Sent Per Day, Week, Month—Per Rep, Sales Team	See above.
Deals	Closed Won	Track the total number of closed won deals in your CRM
	Closed Lost	See above.
	Deal Abandoned Rate (Ghosted)	Track deals where the prospect simply disappears and doesn't respond further.
	Deal Velocity (Average Sales Cycles)	Track how fast deals move through your pipeline. Tools like HubSpot offer this as standard.
	Opportunity to Win Rate Per Rep	Calculate the number of deals opened / the number of deals won × 100 by rep
	Opportunity to Win Rate Per Sales Team	See above.
	Total Sales Per Month Per Rep	Track the total number of closed won deals in your CRM per rep
	Total Sales Per Month Sales Team	Track the total number of closed won deals in your CRM per sales team
	Average Contract Length (Create Numerical Deal Object)	You would need to create a Contract Length property and input once contract secured. Then you would need to set up a Horizontal Bar with Contract Length as the Y-Axis

(*continued*)

(continued)

KPI	Metric	How you get there
	Churn Monthly Per Rep, Sales Team	You could add 'Churned Client' as a lifecycle stage. This then should allow you to create a 'Became Churned Client' filter which you'd be able to monitor on a monthly and annual basis. The report would be a Horizontal Bar with Rep in the Y-Axis and Contact/Company Count in the X-Axis
	Churn Annually Per Rep, Sales Team	Track the total number of churned accounts in your CRM
	Collateral Use Documents	Use document links in your CRM and see how many are accessed and for how long
	Collateral Use Files	As above
	Collateral Use Video	Track all videos watched in the sale process, may require third-party tools.
	Sales Lost to Sales Revenue Ratio	The calculation for this Sales Lost to Sales Revenue Ratio = Total Value of Lost Opportunities / Total Value of Won Opportunities but you also need to standardize closed lost reasons so you can track trends.
Events and Networking	Number of Events Attended Per Rep Per Month	Set up events as a campaign and then track reps attended as a count by rep name

KPI	Metric	How you get there
	Number of Contacts Made Per Event Per Rep Per Month	Track the number of new contacts by events per month by rep
	Number of New Target Accounts Made Per Event Per Rep Per Month	as above but by company and target account if using the function in HubSpot
	Number of Opportunities Made From Events Per Rep Per Month	Track number of deals by deal source "event" per month by rep
	Number of Closed Won Deals Made from Events Per Rep Per Month	Track number of closed won deals by deal source "event" per month by rep
	Number of Accounts Expanded From Event Attendance Per Rep Per Month	Track the number of new deals on current clients where deal source is "event" per month
	$ Value of New Business From Event Contacts	Track the total revenue from new contacts with a deal where deal source is "events"
	$ Value of Expanded Existing Business From Event Contacts	Track the total revenue from current customers with a new deal where deal source is "events" and by company

These KPIs are an ideal place to start, but you can dive deeper than this and we have other individual performance dashboards available through the website support for this book. For example, there are no renewal metrics listed above for SaaS and fintech companies; that's likely a requirement, whereas service organizations may not necessarily need renewals but new deals. Also, some companies may have renewals, cross-sell, and upsell opportunities with their customer success (CS) metrics, so this all depends on how the organization approaches the process. Let's look at our CS metrics to see.

Customer Success KPIs and Metrics

KPI	Metric	How you get there
Retention	Average Customer Lifetime Value	To calculate LTV for a SaaS company, you will need to know the following: Average revenue per user (ARPU): This is the average amount of money that each customer pays per month. Customer churn rate: This is the percentage of customers cancelling their monthly subscriptions. Average customer lifespan: This is the average length of time a customer remains a paying subscriber. Once you have these numbers, you can use the following formula to calculate LTV: LTV = ARPU * (1 / churn rate) * lifespan For example, if a SaaS company has an ARPU of $100, a churn rate of 5% per month, and an average customer lifespan of 36 months, their LTV would be: LTV = $100 * (1 / 0.05) * 36 = $7,200
	Renewals	Track the number of renewals from existing customers with expiring fixed term contracts or subscriptions
	NPS	To calculate NPS, SaaS companies ask their customers to rate their likelihood of recommending the company's products or services to others on a scale of 0 to 10. Customers who give a score of 9 or 10 are considered "promoters," while those who give a score of 0 to 6 are considered "detractors." Customers who give a score of 7 or 8 are considered "passives."

KPI	Metric	How you get there
	Customer Satisfaction Score	To calculate the overall CSAT for a company, the scores from all customers are averaged together. The resulting score is the CSAT, which can range from 0 (all customers are dissatisfied) to 10 (all customers are highly satisfied).
	Net $ Retention Upsells	Track the additional revenue generated from existing customers who upgrade their services or purchase more expensive plans. Calculate by summing up the increased revenue from upsells over a specific period.
	Net $ Retention Cross-Sells	Measure the revenue generated from existing customers who purchase additional products or services. Sum up the revenue from cross-sell transactions over a given timeframe.
	Net $ Retention Downgrades	Monitor the revenue lost due to customers downgrading their services or moving to less expensive plans. Calculate by summing up the decreased revenue from downgrades over a specific period.
	Net $ Retention Churn	Measure the revenue lost due to customers canceling their subscriptions or not renewing contracts. Sum up the total revenue lost from churned customers over a given timeframe.
	Average Revenue Per Customer	Calculate by dividing the total revenue by the number of customers over a specific period (e.g., monthly or annually).

(*continued*)

(*continued*)

KPI	Metric	How you get there
	Canceled Retainers/ Subscriptions	Track the number of customers who cancel their retainers or subscriptions within a given period.
	Closed Accounts	Monitor the number of customer accounts that have been completely closed or terminated within a specific timeframe.
	Loss of Recurring $	Calculate the total amount of recurring revenue lost due to cancellations, downgrades, or churn over a given period.
	Loss of Contract	Track the number of contracts that are not renewed or terminated prematurely within a specific timeframe.
Conversion Rate	Number of Deals Per Account	Calculate by dividing the total number of closed deals by the number of accounts over a specific period.
	Number of Upgrades Per Account	Divide the total number of upgrades by the number of accounts over a given timeframe.
	Number of Form Submissions Per Account	Track the total number of form submissions and divide by the number of accounts over a specific period.
Customer Health Score	Frequency of Contact Per Account	Calculate the average number of interactions (e.g., emails, calls, meetings) per account over a given timeframe.
	Number of Contacts Engaged Per Account	Track the number of unique contacts from each account who engage with your company (e.g., through support, sales, or marketing) over a specific period.

KPI	Metric	How you get there
	Number of Services Purchased Per Account	Calculate the average number of different services or products purchased by each account.
	Total Revenue Per Account	Sum up all revenue generated from each account over a given period (e.g., monthly, quarterly, or annually).
	Net Profit Per Account	Calculate the total revenue minus the cost of servicing each account over a specific timeframe.
Delivery and Account Management	# of client issues resolved per account per month	Track and sum up the number of support tickets or issues resolved for each account on a monthly basis.
	# of hours per target account per employee per month	Monitor and calculate the average number of hours spent by employees on each target account monthly.
	# of tickets past delivery date per employee per month	Track the number of support tickets or tasks that exceed their promised delivery date for each employee monthly.
	# of meetings per account per month by time	Calculate the average number of meetings held with each account on a monthly basis, potentially categorized by meeting duration.
	Account owner NPS Monthly, Quarterly, Annually	Measure the Net Promoter Score specifically for account owners at different intervals (monthly, quarterly, and annually).

(continued)

(*continued*)

KPI	Metric	How you get there
	HubSpot Company Account Score Per Account Per Month, Quarter, Year	Track the HubSpot Company Account Score for each account at different intervals to measure their engagement and success with the platform.
	Labor Utilization Per Employee By Account	Calculate the percentage of billable hours spent by each employee on specific accounts over a given period.
	Processes and Procedures Developed Per Employee Per Account Per Quarter	Track the number of new or improved processes and procedures created by each employee for specific accounts on a quarterly basis.

This set of KPIs for a customer success team makes sense. They cover the main areas you would like to understand like finance, retention, and account health off the bat, and they also focus on employee performance so you can tie the revenue or lack of to the impetus of your employees or lack of. It's an easy group to set up and follow in your service hub or customer success tool. But at ARISE we further customize the service hub to allow you to track employee sentiment. The following metrics are useful for startups with a CRM platform like HubSpot, as larger firms will likely invest in HR tools with or without the facility to track sentiment, but scaling firms could do well to use it. Hear me out, with all of its automation, you can set up enrollment or onboarding workflows for new team members that track how well you and they onboarded, then you can track ongoing how they feel during their employment with you. To me this makes perfect sense and allows business leaders to understand how their business feels while tracking performance. Let's look at people metrics.

People KPIs and Metrics

KPI	Metric	How you get there
Retention	Average Length of Employment in Months Per Employee	Set up a start date property and an end date property with date picker functions. Then create a calculation property called Length of Employment (Months) to track the time between start and today's date. Lastly, create another calculation property called Average length of time to calculate the average across all employees.
	Employee Onboarding Score	Create a workflow with tasks attached to tickets with an onboarding pipeline and track each onboarding step as a ticket to be completed and track how each employee performs onboarding against your SLA, which would be your requested onboarding timeframe.
	Employee Happiness Score Per Month	Use an internal NPS survey to create this score, send monthly to employees.
	Employee Health Index	Use an internal performance survey with Green being Good, Yellow Stressed and Red Overwhelmed. Employees who track red should be reached out to for support, those with lengthy yellow followed up with if persists monthly.

(continued)

(*continued*)

KPI	Metric	How you get there
	Number of HubSpot Certifications Per Employee	If you use HubSpot, attach a certification to a task on a ticket and see how long it takes to complete and count completed tasks as a count for your number.
	Employee NPS (Per Employee) & (Per Team)	Use an internal NPS to ask how the company is doing and track responses individually and at the team level.
	Total Number of Employees Per Month	Build a report tracking the total number of employees not at employment ended status by count.
	Number of Training Hours Per Employee	Track the time it takes to complete any training and certifications using tickets and length of time tickets are open by employee.
	Number of 1:1 Completed Per Employee Per Quarter	Set up a meeting type 1:1 and track how many are completed per employee per quarter
	Number of Sick Days Per Employee Per Quarter	Create a custom property for Total sick allowance, another for Booked sick days, and a calculated property that subtracts booked sick days from total sick allowance, then report on a quarterly basis.

KPI	Metric	How you get there
	% of Employees Attaining Personal Development Goals	Set tasks in a personal development queue per employee and allow only team leaders to close them out with a score. The score should be a custom property, potentially a drop down with a company-wide agree scoring system
	Average Time to Fill Open Positions	If tracking and advertising jobs on the company website, you can track how long jobs posted remain open and calculate the average time by total number of employees.
	Ratio of Internal Promotions to External Hires	Set up a custom property for a job advertised that offers either internal or external to Position filled. Track the count of internal vs external and display as a ratio.
	Number of Employees in Key Roles	Create a property for key role Y/N and assign any posted job for a key role with it as Y. Track number of key roles Y closed with number key roles Y open. Use a sum or count display.
	Average Response Time to Employee Queries or Concerns	Use the ticketing system on the service hub to allow employees to raise queries or concerns and track the average time it takes to respond and solve the tickets.
	Internal Job Application Rate	Track the number of employees that apply for advertised roles as a count display.

(*continued*)

(continued)

KPI	Metric	How you get there
	Employee Peer Recognition Rates	Add a recognition option to the ticket submission type and enable employees to submit recognition tickets and track the rates month on month or quarterly.
	Employee Work-Life Balance Score	Use an internal NPS survey to track work-life balance use a grade or simple Green = Good, Yellow = Frustrated and Red = Unhappy alternatively use a scale of 1-10.
	% of Employees Meeting Strategic KPIs for Organizational Goals or Business Objectives	You can use your onboarding scores as well as the additional performance tasks to help calculate this report.
	Total Number of Customer Interactions Per Employee	Report on the number of activities with customer per employee
	# Vacation Days Taken Per Employee Per Month	Track the number of booked holidays taken monthly per employee

By bringing employee performance indicators into your CRM you can clearly tie marketing, sales, and customer success personnel to metrics and understand how well they are performing over time. This will give you a good indication of who may be in need of support, training, or other further development and who may need managing out. You would obviously need to tie one-to-one feedback in, but that's not managed in HubSpot or a similar tool, so that is an additional consideration; however, if you recorded the calls with an AI recorder, the one-to-one sits on the contact record of the employee and you can then use AI to analyze them over time (just a thought, but a worthy one considering where we are headed in the tech space). Next we look at our finance metrics—ten metrics and one KPI.

Finance KPIs and Metrics

KPI	Metric	How you get there
Revenue	Profit	Calculate by subtracting all expenses from total revenue. This includes both operating and non-operating expenses.
	Gross Margin	Subtract the cost of goods sold (COGS) from total revenue, then divide by total revenue and multiply by 100 to get the percentage.
	EBITDA	Add interest, taxes, depreciation, and amortization back to net income. Alternatively, start with operating profit and add back depreciation and amortization.
	MRR	Sum up all recurring revenue from customers for a given month. For annual subscriptions, divide the annual amount by 12
	ARR	Multiply MRR by 12, or sum up all yearly subscription revenue, add recurring revenue from add-ons and upgrades, then subtract revenue lost from cancellations and downgrades
	Cashflow	Calculate by tracking all cash inflows and outflows over a specific period. This includes operating activities, investing activities, and financing activities

(continued)

(continued)

KPI	Metric	How you get there
	Cash on Reserve	Sum up all readily available cash and cash equivalents, including bank accounts and highly liquid short-term investments.
	Quick Ratio	Divide current assets (excluding inventory) by current liabilities. This measures a company's ability to meet short-term obligations with its most liquid assets
	Revenue Per Employee	Divide total revenue by the number of employees. This metric helps assess workforce productivity and efficiency.
	Team Effectiveness Ratio	Calculate by dividing total revenue by the total number of full-time equivalent employees. This metric provides insight into how efficiently the team is generating revenue.

Now for those in the know, tracking cashflow in HubSpot isn't what it was designed for, but more and more tools are being developed to help this, and their Commerce Hub will definitely help if you choose to adopt it in full. Quotes, payments, and subscriptions all capably managed from one tool with data from your customer facing teams makes for a great all-inclusive GTM support platform. As mentioned earlier in the book, check out Databox, as you can connect finance systems to Databox and curate accurate financial reports from both HubSpot and your other third party tools.

Finally, we have been working on a set of KPIs and metrics for tracking the performance of your user interface and user experience. Something useful for both marketing (website) and product teams to think about. This new set of jump-off metrics is still being fleshed out but we are here so far and as we further develop them, the updates will be available in the portal that has the supporting materials for this book.

User Experience KPIs and Metrics

KPI	Metric	How you get there
User Experience	Customer Satisfaction Score (CSAT)	To calculate the overall CSAT for a company, the scores from all customers are averaged together. The resulting score is the CSAT, which can range from 0 (all customers are dissatisfied) to 10 (all customers are highly satisfied).
	Customer Effort Score (CES)	Customer Effort Score (CES) is a customer experience survey metric that helps product teams understand how easy it was for a customer to interact, accomplish a goal, or resolve an issue within a product or website.
	Net Promoter Score (NPS)	NPS is calculated by subtracting the percentage of customers who respond to your NPS survey with a 6 or lower (aka Detractors) from the percentage of customers who answer with a 9 or 10 (aka Promoters).
	Single Ease Question (SEQ)	A Single Ease Question (SEQ) survey gives users a seven-point rating scale to rate the level of difficulty to complete a task on your site—for example, upgrading their account, subscribing to your service, or purchasing your product.
	Time spent on task	The average time taken to complete one task / total time to complete all tasks

(continued)

(continued)

KPI	Metric	How you get there
	Task Success Rate	The number of correctly completed tasks divided by the total number of attempts
	Search vs. navigation	To measure search vs. navigation, you'll need to set users a specific task (or set of tasks) and watch how they complete them. Do they use the search function and recall a keyword that could help them complete tasks, or do they click through your navigation to get the job done?
	User error rate	The number of errors / total number of task attempts
	Error occurrence rate	Total numbers of occurred errors for all users / total number of error opportunities for all users
	System Usability Scale (SUS) Survey	SUS is a survey based on ten questions. The SUS produces a score from 0 to 100 that indicates the perceived usability of a system. Based on research, a SUS score above 68 is above average, and anything below 68 is below average.
	Customer Churn Rate (CCR)	The churn rate formula is: (Lost Customers ÷ Total Customers at the Start of Time Period) × 100. For example, if your business had 250 customers at the beginning of the month and lost 10 customers by the end, you would divide 10 by 250. The answer is 0.04.

So, that's my list of jump off KPIs and metrics for the ARISE GTM Methodology®. The thought process behind it was to find and establish a baseline of metrics that can be built on for your unique business use case. Again, take time to visit the supporting website for more information on KPIs and metrics that are more advanced and for more playbooks that you can import into your HubSpot CRM.

Tools for Tracking and Reporting

CRMs are the right tools to track most of these metrics and KPIs, and HubSpot's integrated platform is a CRM, Sales, Marketing, and Service platform so from that perspective this all stacks up. I'm sure other tech stacks can deliver the same, but as I don't deviate much from the above, except with the other tools mentioned in this book, I'll stay here. Using more powerful analytics tools like PowerBI may make more sense for complex data analysis but ideally, you minimize the use of additional reporting tools or build low-code options specific to your use case. As I keep saying, AI is the future today, and you can get a ton of analysis on first party data managed and presented with OpenAI, Claude, CoPilot, and Perplexity.

All of these metrics and reports I've listed are accessible on the supporting website and can be cloud deployed directly into your own HubSpot platform if you so choose.

18

Building an Effective Sales Process

Defining Sales Stages and Aligning with the Customer Journey

Sales is one of the most important parts of your business. How you approach sales will decide how fast you grow or not; it's as simple as that. In my opinion, even though it's a highly contested one, you should have a plan from day one. None of this "figure it out on the fly" type approach that basically leaves everything to chance and worked well when it was easy to raise funds to reboot the bank balance. With more investors seemingly wanting traction, and I'm hearing numbers in the region of 1 million annual recurring revenue (ARR) being thrown around, bootstrapping will become more prevalent; and even if you do raise, you need to be both fiscally responsible and operationally excellent. A structured sales process therefore benefits from both. I've always run sales in my business, founder-led in that respect, and when I did hire a sales lead what I got back in return was tumbleweeds. When we finally let him go and looked at the performance data, the average length of a sales call was 27 seconds, and if you count the fact that HubSpot starts counting in its dialer when you press call, it is not a lot of action over a three-and-a-half-month period. So I agree up until a certain size, founder-led sales is the way to go, and it also helps

189

if you want to bring in a sales team that you have a well documented process to hand off, because nobody really sells a product like someone who whole-heartedly believes in it. So where to begin?

Well, I have studied many sales models: the challenger sale, the gap sale, HubSpot's inbound sales process, and certified both MEDDIC and MEDDPICC which ultimately has helped me close some large deals (the biggest $328k), so I am definitely going to back choosing an approach. To get started let's look at MEDDIC and MEDDPICC as they are both sales qualification processes for B2B tech and therefore widely adopted in SaaS and fintech. First, understand that they are not two separate models; MEDDPICC is an evolution of MEDDIC. Let's break them down for you.

MEDDIC

- **Metrics:** Quantification of the potential gain and, ultimately, the economic benefit
- **Economic Buyer:** Interaction with the person who has decision control on the funds for the purchase order (PO)
- **Decision Process:** Process defined by the company to reach the purchase decision
- **Decision Criteria:** Criteria used by the company to make the purchase decision and choose among options
- **Identify Pain:** Actual pains at the company that would require your product/service to be relieved
- **Champion:** Powerful & influential persons at the company who are favorable to your solution

Darius Lahoutifard, one of the founders of the process, says the MEDDIC framework serves as a practical and memorable checklist for salespeople to gauge their understanding, influence, and advancement in each component within a particular account. By evaluating this MEDDIC checklist, sales professionals can objectively assess the qualification status of their sales campaign and the reliability of their sales projections. The elements that remain unchecked on the MEDDIC checklist will guide the sales team toward appropriate actions in the account, ultimately facilitating deal closure.

What I like about this approach is that you can easily distill sets of questions for each stage of the process and keep your teams aligned to selling the same way, qualifying the same way, and using the same language avoiding messaging mismanagement.

MEDDPICC

MEDDPICC is a trademark owned by Darius Lahoutifard of the MEDDIC Academy and is his extension of the MEDDIC process that is split into two parts, although you execute them together as a single checklist.

- **Metrics:** Quantification of the potential gain and, ultimately, the economic benefit
- **Economic Buyer:** Interaction with the person who has decision control on the funds for the PO
- **Decision Criteria:** Criteria used by the company to make the purchase decision and choose among options
- **Decision Process:** Process defined by the company to reach the purchase decision
- **Paper Process:** Formal procurement process that the customer has defined internally for all suppliers, including security review, legal, purchasing, etc.
- **Identify Pain:** Actual pains at the company that would require your product/service to be relieved
- **Champion:** Powerful & influential persons at the company who are favorable to your solution
- **Competition:** The alternatives that the customer is considering alongside your solution, including another supplier, internal developments, or simply status quo (i.e., no decision)

This list easily explains the process of MEDDPICC, but in Darius's checklist there is one more step that does not follow the acronym, so I removed it and placed it below. The value triangle. In the original checklist this step falls between Decision Criteria and the Paper Process. Beyond that he lists the remaining considerations you need to manage the MEDDPICC qualification process.

- **The Value Triangle:** A visual representation of our value for the client's needs vs our competitor.
- **ROI:** Return on Investment or payback period—How to develop any metrics into an ROI pitch
- **Say No:** Why, when, and how to say no
- **Champion Development:** How to identify, develop, and test champions
- **Objection Handling**
- **MEDDPICC Score calculator**

Lahoutifard says the degree of understanding, influence, and advancement in each of these components within a particular account equips the sales professional with a user-friendly and memorable MEDDPICC FRAMEWORK. Evaluating this MEDDPICC framework yields an impartial appraisal of the sales campaign's qualification status and the reliability of revenue predictions. Any unchecked items on the MEDDPICC framework will guide the sales team towards strategic actions within the account, ultimately facilitating successful deal closure.

What I like about this approach is that it's not about consecutive activities, a step-by-step through each bulletpoint, but rather the ability to know what questions to ask wherever the sales conversation is, although it's highly recommended that you create a sales process that includes setting the agenda for each call so that both parties know what to prepare for. Back in May 2023, I wrote an article on standardizing your sales process and I re-read it considering the current topic; here's how I opened that article. Companies and organizations that sell high-value products or services to other businesses (B2B) need a standardized sales process. Not just to ensure that your sales organization works harmoniously and efficiently, but also because it's:

- a scalable, predictable, and easy way to learn for new hires
- easier to measure which parts of the process work or don't work well
- easier to quickly filter out bad-fit prospects
- timesaving and enables you to qualify out
- a simple, structured and pleasant buying experience for the customer

So I am aligned to a sales process rather than teams operating multiple sales processes within one department. How do you scale that???

Often B2B sales cycles are lengthy, so a documented sales process keeps everyone on target to maneuver your prospect down the funnel. In addition to this, there are often multiple stakeholders (decision-makers) involved, so a well-structured sales process and the right technology can combine to great success.

The world has moved on in terms of technology, however there are still thousands of businesses that haven't. Some are now adopting a Revenue Operations blueprint to organize process and technology, others invest in more sales tech, and many others simply pursue the status quo and not much change is happening at all. Whatever you do, you will do much better if you have a process that you can track, measure, and improve. If you haven't already started applying the ARISE approach and are waiting to finish the book, here's one way of approaching that:

1. **Personas:** Every sales organization needs to have identified their buyer personas and the customer's typical buying process. Top sales professionals will know who buys, who influences, and therefore whom to target.
2. **Prioritization:** By identifying the right opportunities, be that industry, business type or size, revenue, or location—planning to target the companies most likely to buy your product or service keeps your activities lean and fruitful.
3. **Research:** Successful sales reps choose their research areas carefully; be that leading industry reports or newsletters, trigger events on LinkedIn or Google Alerts, or even by connecting with others in the industry.
4. **Preparation:** Being prepared isn't simply a list of procedures to follow. You have to have the right mindset, so listen to sales podcasts or read inspiring sales books.
5. **Routine:** Practice list building Monday, outreach Tuesday and follow up phone calls on Thursday. A good routine helps you refine what works best for you as an individual and leaves room for meetings on Wednesdays and Fridays.

In Chapters 2, 4 and 13 we discuss sales enablement and how you deep dive into this during the Strategy stage of the methodology. You should also have assessed your current sales program in stage one, the assessment stage, and thought about what a new sales program could look like in the ideate stage. In those sections of the book we dive into the mechanics of your sales enablement materials, so I'm not covering this further here. Please review if you need a refresher. What we can explore further is how you can define an aligned sales process with Marketing and Customer Success: pre, during, and post.

Marketing and Sales Alignment

If you want to truly understand how to begin your alignment journey, skip back to the start of Chapter 15. I laid out the map for your new course of action. While the 44 rows I lay out cover everything you need to get into they do not represent the sum total; what's missing is a strategic hiring plan and a clearly defined tech stack. Now throughout the book I have talked about HubSpot, its CRM, and the integrated tools it offers across marketing, sales, and customer support. The ease with which you can scale an integrated GTM using the platform plus the discounts that they offer through their HubSpot for Startups program offer most companies a seamless way to grow. By starting with ARISE, then the steps, and finally the technology, most companies have a roadmap for an entirely redesigned aligned plan. Let's look at the process to align the teams to work toward common goals. It can lead to increased revenue, higher sales win rates, and improved customer retention.

The statistics show that:

- 50% of sales time is wasted on unproductive prospecting—but sales reps ignore 50% of marketing leads, mainly because they don't think they're good enough.
- Failure to align sales and marketing teams leads to wasted budget and resources as up to 60–70% of B2B content is not being used, and close to 75% of marketing leads never convert into a sale.

- Working together, these teams can generate 32% higher revenue, retain 36% more customers, and achieve 38% higher win rates.

So what does this look like specifically?

- **Team efficiency and performance:** Aligned teams are 67% more efficient at closing deals. They also save 30% on their customer acquisition cost—and those have a 20% higher lifetime value (MarTech Alliance).
- **Improved customer experience:** Development of a more seamless customer experience. Sales teams can better understand their clients and offer more personalized solutions by utilizing marketing's insightful consumer wants and preferences data.
- **Revenue growth:** Collaboration leads to developing a more effective sales funnel. Businesses with this alignment can generate more than 200% revenue growth from marketing tactics and experience 24% faster growth in revenue (MarTech Alliance).
- **Messaging consistency:** They develop constant messaging that appeals to customers at all stages of the buying journey. This drives credibility and trust among customers, leading to loyalty, which drives sales and retention.
- **Improved data analysis:** Collaboration leads to the effective gathering and analysis of customer data as insights are drawn from a place of common goals, and information is shared freely.

Picking up some of this from an article I wrote on my blog back in April of 2023, we can walk through steps teams can take to bring this together. The first step is to spend time together as a group and build real working relationships, maybe try some competitive sports themed nights out, happy hour, industry events, just go as a team, work as a team, and build some solid old fashioned real-life relationships. What you'll get from this is "shop talk," and teams can start to understand each other without it being forced upon them in a workshop environment. Then move to education. Relationships are a great start, but more important is educating each team member on their opposite's customer understanding. This allows you to create an aligned customer journey rather than an experience that is more akin to a relay team where one passes the baton to another. In an aligned world, marketing, sales, and customer success operate like a football team; there isn't a handoff.

- Sales are the attacking team members
- Customer Success defend any loss
- Marketing call the plays keeping all team members tightly knit and focused operating mostly in midfield between the other teams

It's a common analogy so I am sure you have heard it before. In reality, what you want to see from a combined team effort is marketing sitting in on sales and support calls so that they can learn how prospects behave in the sales process, what they talk about, what their fears and rejections look like, and the problems and frustrations that customers talk about to the support team. This helps shape messaging and marketing content and should also be the point where product teams join the conversation. Today's marketplace has changed from the pre-COVID era, and much like in any other relationship based model, having a team that produces the goods and services tightly tucked away from any customer or financial understanding makes absolutely no sense. If you are building a product or service tool, then your job is to understand the customer start to finish.

Another step these teams can take to align is to design the sales process and sales enablement materials together, because a deeper understanding of the customer and each other develops. This means a heck of a lot more communication. There should be regular meetings to communicate customer feedback, what's working, what isn't, and finding solutions cross-functionally, not to mention identifying and setting shared goals, OKRs, KPIs, and metrics. Shared KPIs can include:

- Cost per lead
- MQLs and SQLs
- Customer retention
- Cost per customer acquisition
- Marketing ROI
- Sales revenue

It's also a great time to understand skills gaps. Both teams should be good at generating insights; collectively they should be a powerhouse. By pairing sales, marketing, and success people together, you can help the organization build a winning collaboration of shared insights adding true strategic value. To identify your skills gap, ask the right questions:

- What are the individuals on your team great at?
- Where could they use support?
- What skills are you lacking completely that would make an impact?
- How does the addition of these help the business achieve their goals?

If you can provide the training cross-functionally then this will further deepen your team's understanding of the customer and the methodologies for attracting, closing, and retaining customers. Finally, you have to address the tech stack. We know about HubSpot, but what other tools are available to you?

Implementing Sales Enablement Tools

- Leadfeeder/Leadinfo: a tool for deanonymizing website traffic
- Hotjar: for showing you how users navigate your website or app
- Cognism: for obtaining contact information
- Apollo: for identifying and contacting companies seeking products or services like yours
- Breeze.ai: HubSpot's engine for identifying companies looking for products like yours
- Clay: for sourcing data for customer acquisition program and data enrichment
- Gong: for sales performance optimization

There are thousands of tools available, and I mean tens of thousands so I cannot list them all, but these tools are widely adopted at this time and they provide data that HubSpot does not, so they complement a HubSpot centered approach. Additionally, I left out many other larger tools like 6Sense and DemandBase which are account-based marketing tools. The space is too wide to discuss in depth, but what I wanted to do was put something together to make it easy to see how your GTM can be effectively engineered to deliver cross-functional results. For example, if I were a startup today, early stage, I'd opt for a HubSpot free CRM or starter, and Apollo sales seats with intent data and connect the two. I'd go for the Marketing and Content bundle on HubSpot for AI support in marketing outputs and if I had one or two customer success reps, two Service Hub seats so I can automate onboarding and customer support. I might also throw Clay in there for the data collection. That tech stack isn't going to burn your budget, depending on the size of your team.

If I were scaling my company I'm all-in on HubSpot, caveat that I am actually building a tool that helps optimize HubSpot adoption in the B2B space. Knowing what I know about GTM and starting with the end in mind, I would apply to the HubSpot startup program and go all-in from the start. However, scaleups love RevOps, so all-in on HubSpot, add Clay and Gong if you don't already have them, and you could opt for Apollo or Cognism, depending on your budget.

In the enterprise space HubSpot still has challenges, namely Salesforce, but they are gaining ground. For platforms and services with high annual contract value (ACV) the account-based approach is normal, and if you are running HubSpot you will also add RollWorks, DemandBase, 6Sense and the enterprise tools that help target key accounts. I've used Rollworks in the business and with my customers and I find it a good tool. One tool I purposely left out is Bombora, they supply the intent data to most of the tools that carry that information, but RollWorks has its additional intent engine, albeit it's a tool best used in the USA, not so much in Europe. They often recommend N.Rich, a European product making ground in the ABM space.

Now you understand why I didn't want to go too broad with tech suggestions as it would be insurmountable for this book at this time. But do check out my list of tools in the back of the book with writeups.

19

Developing Customer Onboarding Strategies

IN THIS CHAPTER we will focus on onboarding. It is widely known that churn can often be attributed at the point of signing a contract. Research shows that when customers sign high-value contracts, around 68% of them immediately feel some sort of buyer's remorse, and a poor hand-off between sales and customer success can effectively kill the renewal before the relationship has truly started. The reason for this typically comes down to personal equity or political capital. Most decision-makers have an amount of political capital that they earn during tenure and each time they enter into a buying arrangement, they expend some of that capital, so a nervy period during handoff can force your buyer back into the trenches, and if comes to them or your solution, they will always protect their interests over yours. So beware, handoff and onboarding are critical to your success no matter what anyone else tells you. Make your buyer look bad and you are out. Also something else to consider, internal politics play a key part in careers; your poor handling of the handoff could give your buyers' internal political opponents power to reduce the buyers premium in the eyes of their peers. So, your messy onboarding may seem trivial to you, but try to stop focusing on your own wants and needs and understand that buying software and services has internal challenges often unrelated to the product itself.

High-touch vs. Low-touch Onboarding

There are two common forms of onboarding. High-touch and low-touch onboarding are two distinct approaches used by companies to guide new customers through the process of adopting and deriving value from their products or services. These strategies shape the initial customer experience, which can significantly impact long-term satisfaction, retention, and overall success.

High-touch onboarding involves personalized, hands-on guidance from human representatives or service agents. It typically includes dedicated support, customized training, and frequent interactions between the customer and a customer success manager (CSM) or team. This approach is often employed by complex products, high-value accounts, or situations requiring significant customization and handholding.

On the other hand, low-touch onboarding, also known as tech-touch, relies more on self-service resources and automated guidance. It leverages technology to provide a scalable, efficient onboarding experience through documentation and knowledge bases, tutorials, in-app cues, and automated communications.

Companies typically choose between these approaches (or a combination of both) based on factors such as the complexity of the product, customer segments, available resources, and scalability requirements. High-touch onboarding can build stronger personal relationships and increase satisfaction for complex products or high-value customers, while low-touch onboarding offers cost-effective scalability for simpler products or broader customer bases.

The choice between high-touch and low-touch onboarding is based on striking the right balance between providing personalized support and scaling operations efficiently to ensure customer success and drive business growth. Here's a comparison of the two models:

High-touch Onboarding

High-touch onboarding involves personalized, hands-on guidance from human customer success representatives. Here are key points that you should consider:

- **Dedicated Support:** Customers are typically assigned a dedicated CSM who provides one-on-one assistance.

- **Personalized Guidance:** CSMs offer customized support, training, and resources tailored to each customer's specific needs and goals.
- **Frequent Interactions:** Regular check-ins, calls, and meetings are conducted to ensure customer progress and address any issues.
- **Complex Products:** Often used for products or services with steep learning curves or those requiring significant customization.
- **High-value Customers:** Typically reserved for high-value accounts or customers with complex needs.

The benefits of the high-touch onboarding approach is that it builds stronger customer relationships, increases customer loyalty allowing for faster issue resolution, and provides valuable customer feedback. The downside is that it becomes resource heavy as your business scales which adds a lot of cost and it may not be feasible for all customer segments.

Low-touch Onboarding

Low-touch onboarding relies more on self-service resources and automated guidance. Here are the key points to remember:

- **Self-service Resources:** Customers primarily use documentation, tutorials, and knowledge bases to learn the product.
- **Automated Guidance:** In-app cues, email sequences, and chatbots guide users through the onboarding process.
- **Minimal Human Interaction:** Direct human support is limited and usually provided only when necessary.
- **Scalability:** Designed to efficiently onboard a large number of customers without requiring proportional increases in support staff.
- **Simpler Products:** Often used for more intuitive products or those with a shorter learning curve.

The benefits of the low-touch onboarding process is that it's cost-effective, scalable, and allows the user to retain control of their experience and learning while freeing up resources in the business to apply to other areas. Although a hands-off approach to onboarding can lead to frustration in finding quick answers for customers with any accessibility issues or if the product user experience and time to value is more complex than you think it is.

For those familiar with product-led growth (PLG), you can see the hallmarks of this business model with low-touch onboarding. For products with freemium self-serve motions, low touch and guided onboarding often make more business sense than carrying human headcount as you do with high-touch onboarding. However, I have seen plenty of self-serve companies make the same critical error with their guided onboarding and basically drag the unsuspecting customer through as many as 27 steps around the products feature dashboard. The job is not to force the user to see everything you have on offer; it's to establish what value they want from your product and get them to it as quickly as possible.

When I worked with a fintech startup called Hibooks, their onboarding process was excessively long at 27 steps. They were aware they needed to optimize that process, and they had made the cardinal sin of wanting the user to see everything they had on offer. And to be fair to them, they had some smart uses of APIs in their onboarding process, but they just hadn't started the segmentation process. After I had the exploratory call with the team, I dug into the onboarding process to experience it for myself. Armed with this learned experience, when they came to my offices I kicked it off by screenshotting and printing each page in silence. They got the message quite quickly and we moved on from there. They knew there are three things users can to do in the product: set up a company, raise an invoice, or scan receipts. So rather than opt for the full 27 step rundown, we moved the decision making process down to six steps by allowing the user to choose what they wanted to do first and then guide them through to the desired value before encouraging them to explore further. This is a simplified version of the events and I'll share more in the case study section in a few chapters, but it gives you food for thought.

Choosing the Right Approach

Many companies use a combination of high-touch and low-touch strategies, tailoring their approach based on factors such as:

- Customer segment and value
- Product complexity

- Available resources
- Customer preferences

For example, a company might use a low-touch approach for its basic tier customers while providing high-touch onboarding for enterprise clients or those with more complex needs. The goal of the business is to find the right balance that ensures customer success while efficiently using company resources. So why don't we explore onboarding playbooks and best practices.

Best Practices for Onboarding

Now I believe that if you want the best low-touch onboarding experience, you model it on a high-touch one. Where there would typically be human engagement, substitute it with video, so it scales. It also feels more human. When using tools like HubSpot's Service Hub or Intercomm, tools of this caliber, email automation and human interaction can be a seamless experience, catering to any of the three models:

- Low-touch
- High-touch
- Hybrid

You can then choose a model and quickly move to create the best experience possible. HubSpot and Salesforce are quickly moving into the AI-Service agent space and allowing their customers to use AI in their chatbots to try and solve problems quickly. The Service Hub by HubSpot is the tool I know best; I've had no use of Salesforces service tool and minimal use of Intercomm so I can't really break that down either. But as a user of the Service Hub in my business, I can attest to the consistent product updates providing a lot of useful power, features and benefits. But before I do that, let's consider the types of onboarding playbooks and frameworks you can adopt.

Digital Onboarding

Digital onboarding requires tools. I can think of Chameleon and Storylane off the top of my head and both have their unique differences and overlap. While I'm not recommending tools in this space, what I will talk about is how you use them.

For instance, I've already said that you really don't want to force users into long dashboard walkthroughs with features they'll forget while they focus on getting to the value they seek. One way to do this is to use Storylane. You can simply record multiple walkthroughs of your software platform and place them on a page of your website and track who uses the tool so that your sales team can identify who to reach out to once they've engaged with a digital demo. Additionally, by having the ability to record multiple variations of the value your offer, having the all-inclusive walkthrough as a choice makes sense.

What Chameleon offers is what happens inside the product, the wizard walkthroughs, the tooltips, surveys etc. Again, even though you can walk people through the product once they log in, realistically you want to employ Chameleon to offer checklist onboarding as it's typically proven to raise adoption rates. So rather than show users what you do, get them to do the thing as they go so that they digest the functionality and you can have them "tick off" each element as they walk through to the desired functionality you asked them about when they first started.

You can then back this up with a tool like Service Hub, where tickets, chatbots, and automated email sequences can be used to help provide support to the user with links to people where necessary and to the knowledgebase when truly self-service. A more low-fi, but still digital solution may be relying on email sequences to run your onboarding; not as sophisticated, but sometimes what's in budget. In that case you would likely have a standard sequence that could look like this:

- Introductory email: The handoff from sales to marketing explaining what comes next
- Welcome email: The email from the account manager or support team explaining how the onboarding process will be run
- Email series: Use email sequencing to provide product value ensuring you have shared how to best get value from your product based on various scenarios
- Support email: Tell your users where they can get support and for what type of issue. This helps them understand your landscape and navigate through
- Triggered Email: Use features to trigger email sequences for complimentary features or upgrade features that may also be useful

- Lack of activity: Use action based triggers to send automated emails to users who haven't accessed the product for some time
- Check in: After around a week in the sequence check in with a support rep or an carefully crafted email that may link to a feedback survey if fully self serve
- Upsell/Cross-sell: If appropriate and the feedback is good, try a free trial upsell to encourage wider adoption of your product

This is a very simple workflow and doesn't really allow for a true onboarding experience. In my mind, and based on my own product usage and adoption (and I am only one) you should aim to onboard over 90 days. I constantly see a 7 or 14 day trial, even monthly; I rarely get to use the product and mostly ask for an extension, although it doesn't always work. I think you SaaS and fintech firms need to offer pauses in the onboarding so that the experience feels aligned to my availability and not the other way around. Imagine how personalized you could make the onboarding to your tool feel, if you just offered a time based pause, irrelevant of the length of time. So don't attack it by asking would you like to pause for 7, 14, 21, or 30 days, just ask them and take the time period and ask why. The cumulative answers to the why, segmented by user type, function, seniority, and industry would give you so much more useful data that a pre-defined timeframe, even if in reality you can only pause for a month.

In-person Onboarding

If your firm is going to adopt hands-on onboarding you better have the right plan. Poorly executed human resources are less likely to be forgiven than digital resources. For high-touch customer success teams, here is an example playbook that you can use to springboard to success:

- Welcome and Initial Setup
  - o Send a personalized welcome email within 24 hours of sign-up.
  - o Schedule a kickoff call to discuss the customer's specific goals and needs.
  - o Create a tailored success plan outlining milestones, tasks, and KPIs.

- Onboarding Checklist
  - o Account setup and configuration
  - o User profile creation
  - o Integration with existing systems
  - o Data import (if applicable)
  - o Custom feature setup based on customer needs

- Training and Education
  - o Conduct personalized product demos focused on the customer's use case.
  - o Provide interactive walkthroughs of key features.
  - o Offer one-on-one training sessions for complex functionalities.
  - o Share tailored resources such as video tutorials and documentation.

- Milestone Check-ins
  - o Schedule regular progress review meetings (e.g., weekly or bi-weekly).
  - o Track completion of onboarding checklist items.
  - o Address any challenges or roadblocks promptly.

- Adoption and Engagement
  - o Monitor user activity and feature usage.
  - o Provide proactive guidance on underutilized features.
  - o Offer advanced training on more complex functionalities as needed.

- Feedback and Optimization
  - o Conduct surveys at key points in the onboarding journey.
  - o Schedule a 30-day review to assess overall progress and satisfaction.
  - o Continuously refine the onboarding process based on customer feedback.

- Transition to Ongoing Support
  - o Introduce the customer to their dedicated account manager or customer success team.

o Provide information on available support channels and resources.
o Set expectations for future check-ins and ongoing relationship management.

This example outlines how you could approach your hands on onboarding program. It does leave a little to you to figure out and so I also wanted to add this seven-step approach that fleshes an alternative program out in more detail.

Step 1: Pre-Onboarding Preparation

Research and Planning:
- Conduct preliminary research on the customer's industry, needs, and goals
- Create a tailored onboarding plan with specific milestones and KPIs
- Assign a dedicated CSM to the account

This step is key especially if your audience is segmented and you have multiple user types.

Initial Outreach:

- Send a personalized welcome email reiterating the customer's goals and purchase decision
- Schedule a welcome call or kickoff meeting

Step 2: Kickoff Meeting

Agenda:
- Introduce the customer success team
- Review the customer's objectives and success criteria
- Outline the onboarding process and timeline
- Address any immediate questions or concerns

Agendas are a great way of setting expectations and provide a lot of value for prepping for calls. It allows your customer to prepare any questions they might have and your customer service rep to focus on a segmented playbook.

Follow-up:

- Send a recap email summarizing key points and next steps
- Provide access to relevant resources and documentation

Step 3: Implementation and Training

Custom Setup:

- Configure the product to meet the customer's specific needs
- Integrate with existing systems if necessary

Some companies charge for high-touch and so this step is based on the complexity of the products adoption. Guided onboarding through weekly calls vs. done for you carry different values to a buyer and you should monetize accordingly.

Training Sessions:

- Conduct interactive workshops or virtual product tours
- Provide hands-on training for key features and functionalities
- Offer role-specific training for different user groups

Step 4: Milestone Check-ins

Regular Touchpoints:

- Schedule weekly or bi-weekly check-in calls
- Review progress towards established milestones
- Address any challenges or roadblocks

While regular check-ins are great, remember to encourage your user to send advance questions so you can address them quickly and efficiently on your next call.

Feedback Collection:

- Gather feedback on the onboarding process and product usage
- Make adjustments to the onboarding plan as needed

Step 5: Advanced Feature Adoption

Personalized Guidance:

- Introduce advanced features relevant to the customer's goals
- Provide use case-specific examples and best practices
- Offer additional training or resources as needed

Step 6: Success Validation

Goal Achievement Review:

- Assess progress towards the customer's initial objectives
- Showcase ROI and value realized
- Identify opportunities for expanded usage or upsells

Customer Satisfaction:

- Conduct a comprehensive review of the onboarding experience
- Address any outstanding issues or concerns

Step 7: Transition to Ongoing Success

Long-term Planning:

- Develop a roadmap for continued success and growth
- Set new goals and KPIs for the next phase

Relationship Handoff:

- Introduce the ongoing customer success team (if different from onboarding)
- Prioritize a smooth transition of knowledge and relationships

Throughout this playbook, the CSM should maintain frequent communication, provide personalized support, and be ready to adapt the process based on the customer's unique needs. Automation tools can be used for task reminders and follow-ups, but the focus should remain on delivering a high-touch, personalized experience.

However, if you want to truly build a winning customer onboarding program, use the service design workshop as a basis for it as it is completely focused on building a winning customer experience.

20

Reducing Churn and Increasing Customer Retention

IN THIS CHAPTER, I want to discuss how you can focus on identifying and mitigating churn.

Identifying Churn Risk Factors

In previous chapters I have discussed churn, account health scoring, and the need to align the customer teams around a single toolset. Never more important is that than at this point in the customer lifecycle. I also pointed out that the point of churn can effectively occur at the time of contracts being signed due to a poorly planned handoff between sales and customer success. But that alone isn't going to solve your challenges.

In the book is a diagram (Figure 1.1) I created showing how the company works to deliver the business plan. On the bottom row on the far right is a box that reads Product User Data. For tech platforms, this is where your company will start to identify churn signals. Off of the top of my head I can think of several that make sense:

- A lack of recent sign-ins
- A rise in user complaints
- A negative contraction in Net Promoter Scores (NPS) and Customer Satisfaction Scores (CSAT)

- Your customers showing up in intent data looking at your rival products
- A poor customer experience
- A poor customer health score
- An advanced request to reduce annual contract value (ACV)

All of the above are indicators that you should track to grasp how well the product is performing against the needs of the client. Let's look at each of them separately.

A Lack of Recent Sign-ins

Tracking user log in data is a crucial task for any Saas or Fintech product. If you start to see a long-term or rapid decline in users signing in to your product, that should trigger an account warning with your CSM or automated process if self serve. While seasonal trends like holiday periods could play a part, the job is to be on top of this activity and feed it back to the CS teams so they can take appropriate action. In a digital environment, make sure you have trigger sequences built into your product based on a lack of sign ins, and include a quick questionnaire to discover if the absence is product related.

A Rise in User Complaints

A rise in user complaints is never a good sign. Often companies in long-term contracts start raising more complaints ahead of time because they are preparing for life without you. In some cases you may find that it's a play for a discount due to their own circumstances but if those complaints spill out of internal tickets into online feedback, the long-term impact on your brand equity can be immeasurable. Ensure you have a strong but achievable service level agreement (SLA) on dealing with client complaints and always be prepared to give to bring the customer back onside.

A Negative Contraction in NPS and CSAT

NPS and CSAT should be more than a token gesture at your firm. Strong scores from your customer base are great but strong scores with commentary on why is much better. Context to your positive or negative scores is incredibly important to understanding the value customers get from your product. There have been many times I have worked with product teams and they don't use either, or when it is done, it's through a manual Google Doc or something similar; nothing that can provide ongoing value to internal teams to provide a better service or improve features.

Your Customers Showing Up in Intent Data Looking at Your Rival Products

While reducing churn is often relegated to the customer success team, in reality it's a whole of company priority. And having a shared view of your customer is imperative to retaining customers, cross-sell, upsell, and to see if they are actively exploring your competitors. With tools that integrate intent data, it could pay dividends to track current customers and have your tech stack ping the CS team when a current customer spikes for a competitor search. You have to be deliberate to do this as most companies use intent in sales and marketing alone.

A Poor Customer Experience

A poor customer experience doesn't need explaining to anyone. Understand that your customers' experience is their experience; you have to accept that is how it is. It's like communication matters so much because words count. So when your customer raises a complaint about your service, don't get defensive and spout how you have X, Y, and Z and therefore "other" people are okay, because you have to treat all complaints individually. When you don't people get pissed.

I canceled my locker at the gym; it was a false economy as I live a seven minute walk, so totally unnecessary. I go in and cancel the locker off of my subscription, and the next month, they try and bill me for it. I raise it with the manager, who says speak to head office, who says to speak to the manager and already I'm annoyed. This is also all happening now by email, another pet hate (yes I want to talk to someone), and after a week I pay the membership without the locker fee. I then receive a ticket from the support team telling me that my locker fee has been canceled from the following month, to which I reply that I canceled last month, and this month isn't due for billing. This is long to read; imagine this has taken days in the real world. So anyway, I go back to the ticket and say hey, this month shouldn't be on the bill, I cancelled last month; to which they reply yes, we are writing off this month's fee from your account so it's all sorted.

Now I don't know about you, but writing off a fee that doesn't exist cannot be right. If you hire something monthly then when you cancel the contract expires too; therefore, you cannot write something off that doesn't exist in the first place. But while some of you may think that it doesn't matter, the bill was canceled, let me tell you it does. Not just because I want to be right, but because down the line if something similar happens, they'll look at the historical view of my account and potentially accuse me of messing around, and not refund me when I was in the right in the first place.

A Poor Customer Health Score

HubSpot's service hub, a tool I use at ARISE GTM, has inbuilt customer health scoring. With this functionality you can combine datapoints together to gain a better understanding of how companies engage with your business. Datasets you can consider are:

- 1:1 Engagement
- 1:1 Call Engagement
- Supported Tickets
- CSM Sentiment
- NPS
- Product usage
- Customer feedback
- Marketing engagement
- Website activity
- Product upgrades and renewals
- Community participation

This list isn't exhaustive, but it does get you thinking about how you mitigate the risk of churn using integrated technologies.

An Advanced Request to Reduce ACV

If your CS or sales team receives an advance request to reduce annual contract value, then that is a sign that something is wrong. In my experience there are around six or seven reasons clients go down this road:

1. Lack of Understanding
2. Budget Constraints
3. Perceived Lack of Value
4. Market Comparisons
5. Previous Success with Negotiations
6. Changed Circumstances
7. Lack of Demonstrated Return on Investment (ROI)

If we look at each of the above separately in context to this discussion, they are all driven by a poor sales process, let alone the handoff.

Lack of Understanding

Many customers don't fully grasp the value of the services or products they're receiving. They might question the necessity of certain features or services, especially if they've managed without them in the past. For instance, a client might ask, "Why do I need a Project Management Tool? I can just use my email or Google docs." This can happen if you don't get the product adopters and decision makers on calls during the sales process. The lack of expansive product knowledge across the buyers organization can hamper renewals through a lack of understanding around the original purchase.

Budget Constraints

Financial pressures often drive customers to seek cost reductions across all their expenses, including service contracts. This is particularly common in industries where cost-cutting is the norm. In SaaS and fintech, this happens a lot, especially when the market turns or sales quarters are down. However, if the product is a nice to have and not a need to have, unless you can portray why the value should remain high, you will be forced to reduce fees at renewal.

Perceived Lack of Value

If customers don't see tangible benefits from the services they're paying for, they're more likely to question the contract's value. This can happen when:

- The impact of the service isn't clearly visible
- The customer hasn't experienced any significant issues that the service has prevented or serves
- The full range of services provided isn't being utilized or understood

Product adoption is another key metric for churn. Sign ins are easy to spot. But unless you are tracking it, you can't see how expansive the product is being adopted internally. This is a common blind spot for early-stage companies.

Market Comparisons

Customers may request lower rates if they believe competitors are offering similar services at lower prices. This perception, whether accurate or not, can lead to pressure for price reductions. Expect this at negotiations and renewals, but it can also be used as a way to get out of a contract without declaring any internal financial reasons.

Previous Success with Negotiations

Some customers habitually ask for discounts because it has worked for them in the past. They may view it as a standard business practice to always negotiate prices. Most companies offer discounts; it's how the world is today as some revenue is better than no revenue. However, in some cases not offering further reductions can cause clients to jump ship.

Changed Circumstances

A customer's needs or financial situation may have changed since the original contract was signed, leading them to reassess the value of the services. This is why with high-touch onboarding, it's impor-tant to temperature check the customers business as well as the use of the product or service. Leading indicators are better than lagging indicators in this case.

Lack of Demonstrated ROI

If your team hasn't effectively communicated or demonstrated the ROI for your product or services, customers may struggle to justify the expense. To address these issues, here's some things to consider:

- Clearly explain the pricing structure and the value provided.
- Regularly demonstrate the tangible benefits and ROI of your product(s) or service(s).
- Offer case studies or testimonials from similar clients who have benefited from the services.
- Consider alternative pricing models or service packages that might better align with the customer's needs and budget.
- Maintain open communication to proactively understand and address the customer's concerns

By addressing these underlying factors, you can often mitigate requests for churn or discounted pricing and maintain mutually beneficial relationships with your clients.

Proactive Retention Strategies

The best proactive retention strategy starts with research. If you are pre-product, run interviews with users of products like yours, and learn what they don't and do like about the customer services. Pay for this information if you have to; contextual relevance is gold dust. Then use tools like G2, Capterra, and other feedback platforms to capture the real-time feedback and analyze that ongoing to keep up with how the customer talks about the competition positively and negatively.

If you are already in market then you can adopt the above and use your NPS and CSAT as well as your win/loss, customer support tickets, and voice of the customer program to accurately figure out what is working or what isn't and why. In truth, the most proactive retention approach is one that focuses on continuous improvement, doesn't stagnate, and moves inline with the customer expectation. Here are some examples of proactivity:

Understanding and Meeting Customer Needs

- **Customer Feedback and Analysis:** Regularly collect and analyze customer feedback to understand their expectations and experiences. This can be done through surveys, reviews, and direct communication.
- **Voice of Customer Programs:** Implement programs that actively listen to customer feedback to continuously improve products and services.

Personalization and Engagement

- **Personalized Experiences:** Use data analytics to tailor customer interactions and offers based on individual preferences and behaviors. This can include personalized recommendations, communications, and promotions.
- **Educational Content:** Provide customers with interactive and educational content that adds value to their experience. This can help in keeping them engaged and informed about how to best use your products or services.

Loyalty Programs and Rewards

- **Loyalty Programs:** Implement programs that reward repeat customers with points, discounts, or exclusive benefits. These programs can encourage continued patronage and increase customer satisfaction.
- **VIP Statuses:** Offer special statuses or tiers within loyalty programs that provide additional benefits to high-value customers, enhancing their sense of exclusivity and appreciation.

Proactive Communication

- **Regular Touchpoints:** Maintain consistent communication with customers through newsletters, emails, or push notifications. This helps in keeping the brand top-of-mind and provides opportunities to address any concerns early.

- **Omnichannel Support:** Ensure that customers can reach support through multiple channels, such as phone, email, chat, or social media, making it easy for them to get assistance when needed.

Continuous Improvement

- **Product and Service Enhancements:** Regularly update and improve your offerings based on customer feedback and market trends. This shows customers that you are committed to providing the best possible experience.
- **Pilot Programs:** Test new initiatives or changes in a controlled environment before a full rollout. This allows for adjustments based on real-world feedback.

All of the tactics you employ to get there should include premium support, product feature enhancements and bug fixes in quick time, and multiple support channels—for example on HubSpot's service hub you can connect tickets, email, chatbots, WhatsApp, and forms to a single support inbox offering multiple choices to the user to get the message to your team. Finally, your CS teams should be well versed on how much of a discount or credit they can offer to an unhappy customer. Personally, I would try and offer free extended months of subscription rather than financial discounts because it allows for time to forget "the incident" if it was of a sufficient scale or magnitude. In truth most buyers will still churn if you discount a few months subscription, so adding time on makes more sense, but that's just my opinion. Ultimately, you have to always speak to the customer, always provide a quick turnaround and consistent updates—there's nothing worse than silence when frustration is building for an end user of your product or service.

The great thing about strong customer service is that what you learn can help power sales and marketing as well as the product roadmap. It literally is the beating heart of the customer experience. Taking frustrations, wins, losses, and compiling accurate feedback to those teams helps them get context from the users, and that can then be applied to the new strategy.

PART

VIII

Case Studies and Practical Insights

"Almost all quality improvement comes via simplification of design, manufacturing, layout, processes, and procedures."

—Tom Peters

PART

VIII

Case Studies and
Practical Insights

21

Real-World Applications of ARISE

Case Studies of Successful GTM Strategies Using ARISE

The Reinhart Group—Brand Refresh and Service Productization

Christina and Emmanuel were referred to me by a prospect that I previously pitched, but who had chosen a different supplier in the final decision, so it was unexpected. They are a family run business that offers psychological support services and corporate health and wellbeing support. When we met them, they were engaging with Amazon and a few other corporate and enterprise organizations, but their online brand visual and their lack of appropriate documentation required by these organizations on the RFP process was working against them.

We had a few calls to introduce ourselves and to establish a baseline understanding, but it was evident that they were not quire prepared to move into this space as quickly as they would like to. We introduced them to ARISE, and like most they immediately balked at the amount of work that goes into it; but as we showed the value of the process and outcomes others had achieved, they became open to the idea. So we agreed to refresh the brand online presence and create sales enablement materials for them as well as productize their services as bigger organizations often do. Here are some details on the project.

The Company Profile   Reinhart Group helps purpose-driven business leaders build employee well-being and retention programs that improve culture in line with business values to enable strong growth. They use the latest evidence-based psychological practices and proven playbooks from experienced clinicians to increase productivity and enable cultural change.

The Objectives

- Upgrade the brand to be glossier, standing out in a crowded field and ultimately attracting bigger corporate clients.
- Redesign the company website.
- Boost brand awareness and visibility.

The Challenges

- Market forces and the numerous options available to corporates, most notably any mental health and wellbeing support provided by their medical or insurance policies, challenge the health and wellbeing space.
- Reinhart Group faced lead generation and conversion issues based on its outdated and incomplete brand presence.
- Their messaging focused more on their services than the outcomes they could deliver, leading to some reluctance for in-person and long-term support programs.
- Upmarket brands like Amazon would enter the sales discussion, but the lack of corporate brand and sales materials hampered the discussions.

The Approach   Reinhart Group had an idea of the type of companies they tended to work well with and have success with, but it didn't have a defined Ideal Customer Profile (ICP) or a breakdown of its personas, leading to less focused sales outreach.

We built a sales and marketing strategy that encompassed:

- Service Design Framework
- Persona Workshop

- Messaging Framework
- Buyer Funnel Stages & Tactics
- Buyers Journey Mapping
- Brand Refresh

Through a series of workshops delivered remotely online, we ran through the service design workshop, which opened their vision to the complexities of navigating the health and wellness corporate land-scape. We formalized personas and their ICP based on the companies that they previously worked with and then fleshed out the customer journey based on the same.

Having spent time productizing my own services, of which I am a massive fan, we used the service design workshop to design a customer experience and productize their corporate services, which when we researched the competitive landscape, was common among the larger corporate suppliers. Our situation, however, had to simultaneously manage the corporate and non-corporate clientele within the new brand experience, delicately creating a balance between going too far upmarket and alienating the non-corp clients and staying too far down market to have a lack of visual appeal to the corporate buyer.

We established that HR are often blockers for them, and looked at strategic campaigns to align with HR and enable them to become the hero of the story internally, while also addressing the SME where they typically had relationships with Managing Directors and other C-Suite executives. We then created positioning and messaging frameworks for each persona and used that to build pages that positioned them correctly focusing on outcome based messaging.

The Outcome   Identified core players, drivers, and decision-makers, resulting in a defined ICP, clear persona profiles, and a messaging framework that could act as a solid foundation for future sales and marketing initiatives.

Launched a new website and branding that:

- Had the more upmarket feel they needed to attract larger corporate clients
- Focused on how Reinhart Group could change their clients' worlds

Productized the service offering: We took the standard service offering and productized it through a service design workshop, creating products that aligned with the customer's growth journey; Assess, Initiate, Elevate and Thrive, and made it easy and recognizable to understand what the business offered and to whom.

To check out the updated visuals and messaging feel free to visit them at www.reinhartgroup.co.uk.

The Testimonial

"Paul has gone above and beyond to help us develop a consistent and successful marketing strategy. He personally dedicates so much effort to guiding us and making sure we get value for money. He is genuinely concerned with the success of his clients and it shows."

—Emmanuel Stiels, Co-Founder, Reinhart Group

Now, you may be thinking why are you using such a small company to emphasize your process? The simple answer is because in terms of size, this is a great example of a startup business, and 60% of our work is with startups and scaleups of various sizes. What I wanted to establish is that despite the many times we get told that "We don't want to do that (ARISE)," when you do, you can achieve seismic shifts in brand perception and business presence. Also, this small company sells into large corporates, something again, small startups want to do, but often struggle to.

DSSI Inc., (Directsourcing.com) Now Acquired by Procure Analytics—ABM, SEO and GTM

DSSI is a much larger business, typically selling into companies worth hundreds of millions or billions in turnover. Think car manufacturers, pharma, chemicals, companies of that size that are multinationals. Obviously a whole different category compared to The Reinhart Group to show the use of ARISE at scale.

I was introduced to DSSI and Heidi Humphries, then Executive Director of Sales and Marketing and Amit Mendiratta, Leader in

Source To Pay and Supply Chain Digital Transformation by Roll-Works, an ABM platform we have previously mentioned as we are an agency partner of theirs.

The business had already acquired RollWorks but had decided that they needed more extensive support, and that was how we became part of the conversation. Initially, when we first introduced Heidi and Amit to ARISE, there was some mild resistance, and as we went on to explain how their lack of marketing led them to have no search engine buoyancy and could only be found by direct brand search, something they were sharing with another company of a very similar name. That was only making it far more difficult to prove any value from their marketing as brand search was shared. So we suggested that we first focus on optimizing the website as some of the pages that ranked were more like knowledge base pages rather than valuable service or product pages, and that became a priority.

The project kicked off with the old way we implemented ARISE, which was through a cloud hosted ticket pipeline that we dropped into HubSpot (they already had it). We went on to assess the current state of affairs; website journey, content value, calls to action, blog content, thought leadership and so on. SEM Rush is the tool of choice for this and we used another tool called Answerthepublic .com which provides insights into questions and statements search engine users type into search engines around keyword topics and of course used Screaming Frog to analyze the inner workings of the website and its structure. To Amit's credit, he wasn't doing too bad with the site and worked tirelessly with us to implement the edits and changes on top of his day to day. We finished the assess stage with a full HubSpot and RollWorks audit.

Heidi helped hugely; when I asked for the documented version of the business strategy it was provided, and we now had a strong understanding of where there was room for improvement, where new technologies could be brought in to close the gaps, and how we could potentially move forward as it was evident that content focus was a must. But rather than jump the gun and get into that, we pushed on with the ARISE process. We began a string of online workshops covering personas, customer journey mapping, messaging frameworks, user journey workshop, jobs to be done, and competitive analysis (which uncovered ProcureAnalytics, but the team were unable to say the acquisition was already in play), and content audits. We looked at the tech stack and the current KPIs, which helped build out the ICP, based on the top eight industries they sold into.

We built out segment hypotheses for the identified market segments and conducted persona interviews to close any gaps the team hadn't yet identified. This uncovered vital information about the level of education around the products and services companies like DSSI offered; some potential customers didn't even know AI-enabled tools existed.

Beyond the research, we used the collected information to redefine the GTM strategy focusing on an alignment between marketing and sales activities using SEO, executive advocacy, social media focusing on LinkedIn, and a tie in between the outgoing blog content, LinkedIn posts for the C-Suite, and the ABM program. We built a sales enablement strategy that adapted the use of Apollo with RollWorks and HubSpot to knit this all together. We then agreed on new KPIs, ad campaigns, industry focused segmented outbound email campaigns using intent data, and RollWorks' own intent engine for keywords to trigger outbound messages around keyword search with Cognism providing the contact data for the companies RollWorks demystified in the dark funnel.

In Heidi's own words we were commended on how we came to understand their business, it's goals, targeting, and messaging, so much so that our team were quickly trusted to continue the content output with very little oversight.

From the keyword research we identified hundreds of suitable top, middle and bottom of the funnel opportunities and worked with Heidi to separate the generic procurement keywords with those that solely focused on indirect procurement and the challenges of the target audience. We then were able to feed these back into Rollworks and create industry segmented campaigns that used display ads alongside the SEO and outbound email campaigns, but only targeting the accounts we identified and a catch-all campaign for net new good fit accounts.

As the campaigns progressed over the agreed six month period, we helped DSSI rank for 273 new keywords; in those keywords DSSI has the top share of search among their top 10 competitors, outranking ProcureAnalytics in traffic and rankings in positions 1–3. We also took their website traffic to the highest it had been in the previous six months to more than 14k in March, up from 11k in February. They also saw their average ranking improve from 91 to 68.63, up 21.09%.

The ABM campaigns saw us engage with 53 target accounts in the same period supporting the sales process with several open deals. Note the average sales cycle for DSSI is more than 12 months.

I'll shortly share an excerpt from the interview Heidi kindly agreed to do for the book, but before we do that, below is a copy of the online testimonial from Amit about the work we did.

A Strong Partner in HubSpot Implementation and Growth Strategies

We recently partnered with ARISE to take our marketing efforts to the next level. Our goal was twofold: improve our search engine optimization (SEO) ranking and leverage the HubSpot platform to generate more qualified sales leads for DSSI (www.directsourcing.com). We're happy to report that ARISE exceeded our expectations. From the outset, ARISE impressed us with their in-depth knowledge of HubSpot's capabilities. However, what truly set them apart was their commitment to understanding our unique business model. They conducted a thorough competitive analysis and took the time to delve into our specific needs and goals. This resulted in a customized implementation plan that directly addressed our challenges and opportunities.

But ARISE's expertise extended beyond the software itself. Their team showcased a keen understanding of current marketing trends and how to utilize them within the HubSpot platform. They provided valuable insights into inbound marketing strategies, content creation best practices, and marketing automation techniques—all meticulously tailored to our industry and target audience.

This forward-thinking approach ensured that we not only implemented HubSpot effectively, but also optimized our overall marketing strategy for maximum impact. Throughout the entire process, BIAS maintained clear and consistent communication. They kept us informed every step of the way and readily addressed any questions or concerns. A special shout-out to Paul and Fawn, whose professionalism, courtesy, and unwavering support throughout the project were invaluable.

Amit Mendiratta

Leader in Source To Pay and Supply Chain Digital Transformation

Direct Sourcing, DSSI Inc.

The two case studies are miles apart in scope and requirements, and show the versatility of using the ARISE GTM Methodology® to shift your business to a more customer centric focus that can include productization of services or could include developing a deeper understanding of your customers.

What really stuck out for me and my team was how ready both Heidi and Amit were in being open to participating in something they felt was already done, and being able to be open with us when we drifted off course and renavigated us, always without it coming back to the process being the problem. In fact, there were times when we were told that they were talking about their customers in ways other agencies simply had not dived deeply enough into. I suppose while I can enjoy the pat on the back, I'm always looking for results and being able to clearly articulate them, but it's so much better when your clients advocate for you. So let's jump into the interview, this is a shorter version, to keep it aligned with the content and topic of discussion.

Interview with Heidi Humphries, Executive Director of Sales and Marketing at DSSI (Acquired by ProcureAnalytics)

Paul Sullivan:	Heidi, thank you for joining me today. Could you start by introducing yourself and telling us about your role at DSSI?
Heidi Humphries:	Certainly. I'm the Executive Director of Sales and Marketing at DSSI, which is now part of Procure-Analytics. DSSI is a procurement provider, offering

source-to-pay services primarily to large manufacturers in heavy industrial, food, and pharmaceuti-
cal settings. My role involves understanding how
we present ourselves in the marketplace, identifying what's valuable to our prospective customers,
and packaging our capabilities in a way that resonates with them.

Paul: **Can you give us some background on DSSI and
its history?**

Heidi: DSSI was founded in 2001. Over the years, we've
tried various approaches to marketing and selling,
including attending national trade shows and
aligning with industry-specific organizations.
However, our ownership eventually realized that
these expensive events weren't as effective as targeting companies actively looking for solutions
like ours. This realization led us to focus on engaging potential clients at the exact moment they
were considering transforming their procurement
and sourcing strategies.

Paul: **How was your marketing team structured
before working with us?**

Heidi: For quite a few years, I was a team of one in terms
of dedicated marketing personnel. However, we
had a very tenured executive team with
10–20 years of experience who could contribute
their expertise when needed. My colleague Amit
Mendiratta, our Director of IT, was also instrumental in understanding our processes and where
we could optimize or augment existing systems.

Paul: **What challenges did you face with previous
marketing efforts?**

Heidi: One of our biggest challenges was brand awareness. Despite being in the market for 23 years,
we still encountered people who had never heard
of us. We tried working with various marketing
providers, but found that if they didn't truly

understand our business and value proposition, it was difficult for them to create effective content and reach the right audience. Our experience with previous providers was often frustrating, as we had to spend a lot of time educating them and rewriting their work.

Paul: **How did your experience with ARISE differ from previous agencies?**

Heidi: The approach ARISE took was much more comprehensive. While it initially felt like we were revisiting work we'd already done, such as creating personas and customer journeys, the depth of the process was far beyond what we'd experienced before. You really pushed us to document our tribal knowledge and connect the dots in ways we hadn't before. This allowed you to truly understand our business and provide more valuable insights.

Paul: **Can you elaborate on the persona development process we went through?**

Heidi: The persona development was much more detailed than we'd done previously. We didn't just identify roles and pain points; we delved into the day-to-day experiences of these personas. For example, we created a persona called "Purchasing Paul," who might be hesitant about our services due to fear of being replaced. Understanding these nuances helped us tailor our messaging more effectively.

Paul: **How did our technical approach to content creation differ from your previous experiences?**

Heidi: Your approach was much more strategic and comprehensive. You didn't just suggest topics; you provided specific guidelines on content length, type (like case studies or white papers), and how to link different pieces together. You also had a deep understanding of various marketing technologies and how they could work together in our strategy. This level of technical expertise was invaluable to us.

Paul: What results did you see from our collaborative efforts?

Heidi: We saw significant improvements in our SEO performance. Your help in developing a consistent content strategy, with regular posting schedules and targeted keywords, made a big difference. By the end of our engagement, I was spending minimal time reviewing content because you had such a strong grasp of our messaging and target audience.

Paul: Looking back, how do you feel about the investment of time and effort in the initial discovery and strategy phase?

Heidi: While it was initially challenging and time-consuming, I now see it as absolutely worthwhile. The deep dive into our business was crucial for laying the groundwork for success. It allowed you to fully understand our industry and deliver real value, not just in content creation but in overall messaging and strategy. Your ability to come up with relevant ideas and suggestions was a direct result of this thorough process.

Paul: How did the ARISE Go-To-Market Methodology® impact our work together?

Heidi: The ARISE methodology was a game-changer for us. It provided a structured approach to our marketing efforts that we hadn't experienced before. The framework helped us align our messaging, target the right personas, and create content that truly resonated with our audience. It was particularly effective in helping us navigate the complexities of our industry and communicate our value proposition more clearly.

Paul: Thank you, Heidi, for sharing your experience. Is there anything else you'd like to add?

Heidi: I'd just like to emphasize how impressed I am with your dedication to this book project. As someone who sometimes struggles to see to the end of the week, I'm in awe of your energy and commitment to completing this in such a short timeframe.

For those of you reading that may need indirect spend optimization or wider procurement process optimization, please reach out to Heidi and her team; they are a great resource and deliver concrete results and savings.

Lessons Learned and Best Practices

As with everything I do in life, I see things as part of the journey. I'm a consistent learner, focusing as much on keeping relevant, seeing what's coming over the horizon and relaying that to my teams and clients so that we best prepare for market swings, technical evolution like AI, and other factors influencing brand building and customer acquisition. I read about marketing, sales, customer success and product. It's this approach that help me design ARISE in the first place and it's this approach that keeps me evolving it from swipe files to ticket pipelines and onto SaaS.

Because I'm constantly tied to the ever evolving GTM landscape, it has made me put a stake in the ground and adopt my own position on how you get success, or at least how you do it with ARISE. My experience is that the teams we work with that go all in see results and the teams that don't complete the process well see smaller results. There have been occasions when we sign an ARISE contract with a company, and it feels like they do everything in their power to block us from success. Withhold information, tell us we can perform win/loss, then when you are contracted pull the plug. Some companies have even walked through most of the process, then when we get to the sales enablement piece decide that they have enough from us and that they can take it from there, oftentimes there's not much you can do, especially in the startup world. What I do hope is that with this book and my approach I help a lot more founders and business leaders take the approach and apply it successfully in their own businesses. What I want to emphasize is that if you want best practice then here it is. My answer when you say is all of that necessary I say, yes, it is. Most businesses win in small percentages that deliver large revenues, if you don't get into the trenches to win every now and again, then you're not doing it right.

Remember that this book is about a unified approach that covers strategy, tactics, people, and technology. It's not a checklist, but a series of activities and events that you can perform repeatedly to deliver results. It should feel familiar, not revolutionary but evolutionary and it should always end up with you building or pivoting to a truly customer centric model.

What I don't want to hear from readers of this book after, are comments like "We need to align marketing and sales," it's not that hard, and it's been bandied about far too regularly since the early naughties; it's about time you effected the game differently and started with best practice and the desired outcome in mind.

Growth is a mindset, an inner belief you have to make shit work, come what may, whatever the obstacle. What you have in your hands is a measurable scalable way to move your business forward, with clear direction on some of the best in class tools for your GTM and of course an easy to access support portal with materials that can help those with any budget to adopt ARISE.

I've shared my journey with ARISE. To date, we've pivoted twice in 12 months, both times getting tighter and tighter to the niche positioning we should have, based on the four ways we typically help our customer base. I'm still learning, I have another 12 months to see how our rebrand and service productization is received in the market and discover if we are as good as eating our cake as we are selling it. ARISE has given me a focus I didn't have before and even without a fully-fledged SaaS at this point in time, the way we are using this in our custom build in HubSpot has transformed the way I look at GTM. And I'll happily share a truth with you reader. When I first built the custom objects in HubSpot and then implemented it for my own business, I got tired. GTM strategy and planning is tiring and I crammed four products into one week, with some support from Perplexity.ai and yet I can honestly say I understand why people cut corners.

GTM is hard. It's taxing, it's laborious, but when you do it right and you have the clarity you were always seeking, you do ask yourself the question. Why didn't I do it this way in the first place?

Finally, at least for this chapter I want to say this. As an individual, I'm not happy to accept the status quo, and this can put me at odds with people; and while I am not wanting confrontation, I do feel the marketing community can be a bit vanilla and repetitive. When it comes to the challenges we face, why do we keep spouting the same things? Is it frustration, is it safe to play among the herd, are we fright-ened to challenge the status quo? We should be the drives of change, emboldened to grab the sales bull by the horns and say enough; it's alignment or mediocrity, which do you prefer?

I don't want to hear speakers say the future is AI, it's already here, don't we know it. That's not insight, that's common knowledge. It's the same with alignment and ABM; it's old news, so if we as marketers are prepared to put the same drivel on stage or at roundtables and showcase that as insights, then maybe we get what we deserve; maybe for our lack of true inquisitiveness and willingness to shake up the foundation, dive into the complexities of these things, and share knowledge that enables others to truly shift forward, maybe all we deserve is mediocrity. Me, I can't be in that camp. I do believe the results are in the detail, I do believe we need to be agile, and I do believe we need to do things as formatively as possible. We owe it to ourselves to shape our own destiny. This is ARISE, this is my GTM. What's yours?

22

Common Challenges and How to Overcome Them

WE ARE NOW entering the penultimate chapter of *Go-To-Market Uncovered* and I hope you've found value in the content so far. In this chapter I want to talk to the common challenges companies face in building GTM strategies that make a difference and last long-term.

Addressing Common GTM Challenges

The primary challenge companies face when building a go to market strategy is understanding the target market and the competitive landscape. From early-stage founders to established enterprises, it's not just about knowing who the competitors are, but also understanding how they impact your customer acquisition processes. In addition to this, you should 100% understand the necessity to revenue growth that a deep, clearly identified understanding of each competitor is. Once you understand your customers, your differences, what's done better, worse or differently, and how their online feedback can be used against them in your favor, then your competitive advantage can be leveraged, but additionally you can directly challenge the buyer in the sales process through the use of intent data. Because of data from Bombora fueling tech these days, they can show you companies looking for products and services like you offer. Go to RollWorks, and they can identify companies from keyword search. This means if you use RollWorks in the US, you can literally build a compete strategy by email for each competitor, targeting companies that are visiting their websites. That's a great example of a weaponized compete strategy.

Companies often skip or skim through market research and analysis, getting enough to feel happy with the effort but not enough to be dangerous with it. I've had conversations with Growth Managers who balk at the depth we go to in the market and competitive research part of strategy building and see it as unnecessary. One even told me that they didn't see the point of it. I think competitive analysis easily feeds not only outbound sales and battlecards but gives marketing themes on which to attract new audiences or deter existing ones from considering the competition. It adds fuel to your strategy and opens great opportunities.

Additionally, companies often struggle to stay up to date with market trends and therefore lack insight in what's important and coming over the horizon. By fastidiously focusing on industry trends and gathered insights, you can quickly become the market leader from your content because you understand what your customers seek from products or services like yours. This feeds your competitive advantage and keeps the business moving in the right direction. Finally, all of the above helps with your segmentation and effectively targeting the right audience.

The next challenge is to nail your positioning, messaging, and differentiation. Most companies struggle with this so you aren't alone. Positioning is not a one size fits all process. If you think back to what I said about buying committees, you actually need to be able to position your product or service to the person in the buying process. That's conveying your value, benefits, and differentiation. I also don't believe you can do this solely from the inside out—I mean by doing it all internally without speaking to your customers and then testing your new positioning with them and strangers. Remember for early-stage companies you should use respondent.io for choosing persona archetypes and interviewing them, testing various positioning and messaging statements. For later stage companies maybe Wynter would make more sense. Ultimately this activity should be tied to your voice of the customer program so it becomes a rolling mechanism attached to your long-term strategy.

Common issues for companies in articulating a clear and compelling value proposition are defining what makes the product unique, how the product differentiates from the competition, and as I mentioned earlier, communicating that value to segments within the target audience. If you fail to solve these challenges your poorly defined value proposition will fall on flat ears and hinder the success of your GTM strategy.

Pricing strategy is up next as you can always be leaving money on the table. Earlier in this book we looked at pricing strategies and pricing models; as your product and market develop, new pricing opportunities will develop. AI is going to cause a lot of tools to go bust, with the rapid ability to add further functionality now easily done with AI written code, I don't see nuanced tools making so much of an impact anymore. HubSpot for example could replicate Clay quite easily. It doesn't have to even look or work the same but if they can get the same outcomes for their users, does that bode well for users? Not that I am saying Clay will go at all, it's too big; but all tech functionality is easily copyable with AI, so there's no safety unless you gain a huge market share so that new tools may scratch, but they won't bite your business.

The most common pricing strategies are value-based pricing, flat rate plus usage based pricing, and freemium pricing models. For non PLG GTM models, value based and flat rate plus usage are very common. As with all things, still talk to the customer and non-customers to understand perceived value based on the job the user is hiring the product to solve.

Internal team alignment and collaboration. This, since the turn of the century, the naughties as we say, we've been calling for tighter alignment between marketing and sales. As an industry, there have been too many problems affecting shareholder returns to force companies to adopt best practices in this area. The growth at all costs mindset didn't call for alignment, it just called for revenue and shareholder returns. That being said, while it is entirely possible and plausible to sell your way to success without a marketing engine, those are few and far between. Still, my ARISE GTM Methodology® literally builds this in, so again early-stage founder or late stage scaleup, either way you should build in this way. Ensure your tech stack works for the company, not the champion—that is just because your sales lead says Salesforce that doesn't mean its the best for the business. Whatever happens in the tech stack you want to avoid lots of Zapier or make connections, tech that doesn't integrate easily with customer facing teams. Having teams operating in three separate systems would send alarm bells ringing in my mind unless there's a damned good reason for it, as often there isn't. In many cases it's more a case of "well we started with it and we never changed it."

Data around alignment really stacks up; hence the rapid growth of the RevOps function—companies that align are seemingly 40–60% better off than companies that don't. So firstly, ensure you have a comprehensive GTM strategy drafted between marketing, sales, customer success, and product—see my earlier graphic for this and ensure each clearly understands the other to drive deep internal engagement. Ensure that this isn't a token effort and that regular cross functional meetings are focused on joint outcomes as well as individual outcomes. Once this has been achieved its important that there is an aligned language used (messaging) across the teams so that everybody conveys the same message no matter where they are in the business. When asked "What does your business offer" the answer should be the same. The smallest lack of alignment can result in mixed messaging, which confuses the buyer, conflict and or inconsistency in the buying experience. This increases CAC and churn, which is counterproductive to what this book stands for.

Resources and budgets require proper allocation, and this is vital for a successful GTM strategy. Challenges that your company may face are determining the right mix of marketing channels (paid, earned, owned, and borrowed), which ARISE research helps you uncover. Allocating sufficient budget for various GTM activities, which the assessment, research, and ideation stages help curate, and the strategic phase helps you pinpoint and ensure maximum return on investment (ROI) for marketing and sales efforts. This is solved by data and insights as well as hiring the right people. Under-allocating budgets or over-allocating resources can hinder the progress of your newly defined GTM strategy.

Aligning the product feature roadmap with the customer expectations is another common error in hindering your GTM strategy. Ineffective allocation of resources and budget to ineffective product features can literally pause your ability to grow. Historically there has been many cases of startups veering off course with design partners that take the product away from its core purpose and the run rate significantly suffers. Try as much as you can to listen to the customer, but in a proactive manner, and gauge the impact of a feature and its broad adoption before committing to further development without customer insight.

Finally adapting to market changes or lack of will put a huge dent in your GTM capabilities. Earlier in the book I referenced Bain & Co and the article that discussed what good businesses do when the landscape starts to change. They trim the fat, optimize the spend, and make sure they only have the right people onboard to see them through. Then they go on M&A sprees, which might not be affordable to your company, but the approach is key to your long term success. More of this please reader.

ARISE GTM Strategy for Continuous Improvement

As with any good strategy book, we want to ensure that we don't only cover what you can do to set out, but also what you can do once you're in play. Experimentation is a key driver of success for marketing and sales campaign tactics, so let's dive into situational experiments across the GTM strategy.

Experiments Using Marketing Attribution

1. *Channel Performance Analysis*

Objective: Identify which marketing channels are most effective in driving conversions.

Experiment: Use multi-touch attribution models to analyze the performance of different channels (e.g., social media, email, paid search). For instance, you can compare the effectiveness of Facebook ads versus Google ads in driving sales.

Implementation: Track customer interactions across multiple touchpoints and assign credit to each channel using models like linear, time-decay, or U-shaped attribution.

Outcome: Determine which channels contribute most to conversions and allocate budget accordingly.

2. Content Effectiveness Testing

Objective: Validate the impact of different types of content on engagement and conversions.

Experiment: Conduct A/B tests on various content formats (e.g., blog posts, infographics, videos).

Implementation: Create different versions of a piece of content and measure engagement metrics such as time on page, shares, and conversion rates.

Outcome: Identify which content formats resonate best with your audience and drive higher engagement and conversions.

3. Ad Copy Optimization

Objective: Improve the performance of ad campaigns by testing different ad copies.

Experiment: Run A/B tests on different versions of ad copy to see which one performs better.

Implementation: Create multiple versions of an ad with varying headlines, descriptions, and calls-to-action. Measure the click-through rates (CTR) and conversion rates for each version.

Outcome: Identify the most effective ad copy that drives higher CTR and conversions, and use these insights to optimize future campaigns.

Experiments Using Cost Analysis

1. Pricing Strategy Testing

Objective: Determine the optimal price point for a product to maximize revenue.

Experiment: Conduct A/B tests with different pricing strategies (e.g., cost-plus pricing, competitive pricing, anchor pricing).

Implementation: Offer the same product at different price points to different customer segments and measure the impact on sales volume and revenue.

Outcome: Identify the price point that maximizes revenue without significantly reducing sales volume.

2. Discount Impact Analysis

Objective: Understand the effect of discounts on sales and profitability.

Experiment: Run experiments offering different discount levels (e.g., 10%, 20%, 30%) to various customer segments.

Implementation: Track the sales volume, average order value, and overall profitability for each discount level.

Outcome: Determine the optimal discount level that boosts sales while maintaining profitability.

3. Bundling Strategy Testing

Objective: Evaluate the effectiveness of product bundling in increasing sales.

Experiment: Test different bundling strategies (e.g., bundling complementary products, offering bundle discounts).

Implementation: Create product bundles and offer them at a discounted price compared to purchasing items individually. Measure the impact on sales and average order value.

Outcome: Identify the most effective bundling strategy that increases sales and enhances customer value perception

Optimizing Pay-Per-Click (PPC) Campaigns

Here are several experiments you can run to optimize your PPC campaign effectiveness:

1. Ad Copy A/B Testing

Objective: Improve click-through rates (CTR) and conversions by identifying the most effective ad copy.

Experiment: Create two versions of an ad with different headlines, descriptions, or calls-to-action.

Implementation: Use Google Ads' built-in A/B testing feature to serve both ad versions randomly to your target audience. Run the test for at least two weeks or until statistical significance is achieved.

Outcome: Determine which ad copy version performs better in terms of CTR and conversion rate. Implement the winning version across relevant campaigns.

2. Landing Page Optimization

Objective: Increase conversion rates by improving the landing page experience.

Experiment: Test different landing page elements such as headlines, images, form placement, or call-to-action buttons.

Implementation: Create multiple versions of your landing page using a tool like Google Optimize. Split traffic evenly between the variants and measure conversion rates over a set period.

Outcome: Identify the landing page version that yields the highest conversion rate and implement those changes across your campaigns.

3. Keyword Match Type Testing

Objective: Optimize keyword targeting and improve ad relevance.

Experiment: Test different match types (broad, phrase, exact) for your target keywords.

Implementation: Create separate ad groups for each match type and run them simultaneously. Monitor performance metrics such as CTR, conversion rate, and cost per conversion.

Outcome: Determine which match types perform best for different keywords and adjust your keyword strategy accordingly.

4. Bid Strategy Optimization

Objective: Improve campaign ROI by finding the most effective bidding strategy.

Experiment: Test manual bidding against automated bidding strategies like Target Cost Per Action (CPA) or Maximize Conversions.

Implementation: Split your campaign into two identical sets, applying different bid strategies to each. Run the experiment for at least a month, comparing key performance indicators.

Outcome: Identify the bidding strategy that delivers the best results in terms of conversions and cost-efficiency.

5. Ad Extension Testing

Objective: Enhance ad visibility and improve CTR by utilizing effective ad extensions.

Experiment: Test different combinations of ad extensions (e.g., sitelinks, callouts, structured snippets) to see which ones drive the best performance.

Implementation: Create multiple ad extension sets and rotate them across your campaigns. Monitor CTR and conversion rates for each set.

Outcome: Determine which ad extensions contribute most to improved CTR and conversions, and implement them across relevant campaigns.

By systematically running these experiments, you can continuously optimize your PPC campaigns for better performance and ROI. Remember to allow sufficient time for each test to gather statistically significant data before drawing conclusions and implementing changes. 30, 60, and 90 day experiments work best as you find more optimization within your campaigns.

Optimizing LinkedIn Ad Campaigns

Here are several experiments you can run to optimize your LinkedIn ad campaigns:

1. Audience Targeting Test

Objective: Improve campaign performance by refining your audience targeting.

Experiment: Compare job title-based targeting against job function and seniority-based targeting.

Implementation: Create two identical campaigns, one using job titles + industries, and another using job function + seniority + industries. Run both campaigns simultaneously for at least two weeks.

Outcome: Determine which targeting approach yields better results in terms of lead generation, cost-per-lead, and click-through rate.

2. Ad Format Test

Objective: Identify the most effective ad format for your campaign goals.

Experiment: Compare different ad formats such as Document Ads with Lead Gen forms versus Single Image Ads.

Implementation: Create separate campaigns for each ad format, keeping other variables constant. Run the campaigns concurrently for a set period.

Outcome: Evaluate which ad format performs better in terms of cost-per-click, click-through rate, and cost-per-lead.

3. Ad Copy A/B Test

Objective: Improve ad engagement and click-through rates.

Experiment: Test different variations of ad headlines, descriptions, and calls-to-action.

Implementation: Use LinkedIn's built-in A/B testing feature to create multiple ad variations within a campaign. Rotate ads evenly to ensure fair testing.

Outcome: Identify the ad copy elements that resonate best with your audience and drive higher engagement.

4. Landing Page Optimization

Objective: Increase conversion rates from ad clicks.

Experiment: Test different landing page designs, headlines, and form placements.

Implementation: Create multiple versions of your landing page and split traffic evenly between them. Ensure message match between the ad and landing page.

Outcome: Determine which landing page version yields the highest conversion rate and implement those changes across your campaigns.

5. Bid Strategy Test

Objective: Optimize campaign budget and improve ROI.

Experiment: Compare different bidding strategies, such as manual bidding versus automated bidding.

Implementation: Set up two identical campaigns with different bidding strategies. Start with a higher bid and gradually lower it as you optimize your ad creative and CTR.

Outcome: Identify the bidding strategy that delivers the best results in terms of conversions and cost-efficiency.

By running these experiments alternately, you can continuously refine your LinkedIn ad campaigns for better performance and ROI.

Allow enough time for each test to accrue a suitable amount of data before you close out and move on the next.

Optimizing Audience Segments Across Channels

Here are some experiments you can run to optimize your audience segments across various channels:

1. Cross-Channel Behavioral Segmentation

Objective: Improve targeting accuracy by creating segments based on user behavior across multiple channels.

Experiment: Compare performance of traditional demographic segments against behavioral segments derived from cross-channel interactions.

Implementation:

1. Use an integrated marketing platform to collect data from all channels (e.g., website, email, social media, ads).
2. Create behavioral segments based on engagement patterns, purchase history, and content preferences across channels.
3. Run parallel campaigns targeting both demographic and behavioral segments.
4. Measure engagement rates, conversion rates, and ROI for each segment type.

Outcome: Determine which segmentation approach yields better performance metrics and use insights to refine future audience targeting strategies.

2. Predictive Analytics-Based Segmentation

Objective: Enhance personalization by anticipating customer needs and preferences across channels.

Experiment: Test effectiveness of predictive segments against standard RFM (Recency, Frequency, Monetary) segments.

Implementation:

1. Employ machine learning algorithms to analyze past customer behavior and create predictive segments.
2. Develop parallel marketing campaigns for predictive and RFM segments.
3. Deploy personalized content and offers based on predicted next actions for each segment.
4. Compare conversion rates, customer lifetime value, and engagement metrics between segment types.

Outcome: Assess the impact of predictive segmentation on campaign performance and customer engagement across channels.

3. Cross-Channel Retargeting Optimization

Objective: Improve retargeting effectiveness by optimizing audience segments across multiple platforms.

Experiment:: Compare performance of platform-specific retargeting versus unified cross-channel retargeting.

Implementation:

1. Create two retargeting campaigns: one using platform-specific audiences and another using a unified audience pool.
2. Use a cross-channel analytics tool to track user interactions across all touchpoints.
3. Implement dynamic content adaptation based on previous interactions.
4. Measure conversion rates, click-through rates, and return on ad spend for each approach.

Outcome: Determine the most effective retargeting strategy and use insights to refine cross-channel audience segmentation.

4. Lookalike Audience Expansion

Objective: Expand reach by identifying new potential customers similar to high-value segments across channels.

Experiment: Test performance of lookalike audiences against interest-based targeting.

Implementation:

1. Use data from your CRM and marketing platforms to identify traits of your best customers across all channels.
2. Create lookalike audiences on various platforms (e.g., Facebook, Google, LinkedIn) based on these high-value segments.
3. Run parallel campaigns targeting lookalike audiences and interest-based audiences.
4. Compare acquisition costs, conversion rates, and customer lifetime value between the two approaches.

Outcome: Evaluate the effectiveness of lookalike targeting in expanding your customer base and use findings to refine audience expansion strategies.

As you can see the more you want or need to run experiments, the higher the drive to acquire the correct technology to enable you to execute them. We talk about machine learning here and AI will provide just as effective results, especially the more expensive OpenAI/ChatGPT. Audience expansion experiments typically require Martech or analysis platforms including GA4, Dreamdata.io, PowerBI, and so on. The point is that you have to include them otherwise you run the risk of wasting your budget or misinformation leading to you missing the mark.

Finally, let's look at some of the experiments that sales teams can run to help improve their campaign performance.

Optimizing Sales Performance Across Channels

Here are some experiments you can run to optimize your sales campaign performance across channels:

1. Subject Line A/B Testing

Objective: Improve email open rates and engagement across channels.

Experiment: Test different subject line variations for email campaigns and other messaging channels.

Implementation:

1. Create two versions of subject lines for each campaign.
2. Use A/B testing tools in your email marketing platform to split your audience.
3. Send each version to an equal segment of your audience.
4. Monitor open rates, click-through rates, and conversions for each variant.

Outcome: Identify subject line styles that resonate best with your audience, leading to higher open rates and improved engagement across channels.

2. Cross-Channel Retargeting Optimization

Objective: Enhance conversion rates by optimizing retargeting efforts across multiple platforms.

Experiment: Compare the effectiveness of platform-specific retargeting versus unified cross-channel retargeting.

Implementation:

1. Set up two retargeting campaigns: one using platform-specific audiences and another using a unified audience pool.
2. Use a cross-channel analytics tool to track user interactions across all touchpoints.
3. Implement dynamic content adaptation based on previous interactions.
4. Measure conversion rates, click-through rates, and return on ad spend for each approach.

Outcome: Determine the most effective retargeting strategy to improve overall sales performance across channels.

3. Sales Messaging Experiment

Objective: Identify the most effective sales pitch and messaging across different channels.

Experiment: Test various messaging approaches and copy in sales communications.

Implementation:

1. Create multiple versions of sales pitches and messaging.
2. Allow sales reps to use different versions across various channels (email, phone, social media).
3. Track engagement rates, response rates, and conversion rates for each version.
4. Use tools like HubSpot for mass A/B testing of messaging, including calls and email.

Outcome: Discover the most resonant messaging that drives higher engagement and conversions across channels.

4. Landing Page Optimization

Objective: Increase conversion rates from ad clicks and other channel referrals.

Experiment: Test different landing page designs, headlines, and call-to-action placements.

Implementation:

1. Create multiple versions of landing pages using tools like HubSpot or Unbounce.
2. Direct traffic from various channels to different landing page variants.
3. Monitor conversion rates, bounce rates, and time on page for each version.
4. Ensure message match between ads/referral sources and landing pages.

Outcome: Identify the most effective landing page elements that drive conversions, improving overall sales performance across channels.

5. Multi-Touch Attribution Modeling

Objective: Understand the impact of different channels on the overall sales process.

Experiment: Compare different attribution models to assess channel effectiveness.

Implementation:

1. Implement a multi-touch attribution model using a customer experience and data platform (CXDP).
2. Track customer interactions across all channels throughout the sales funnel.
3. Apply different attribution models (e.g., first-touch, last-touch, linear, time-decay) to your data.
4. Analyze the contribution of each channel to conversions under different models.

Outcome: Gain insights into the most influential channels in your sales process, allowing for optimized budget allocation and improved cross-channel strategies.

Other experiments of course are available, especially when it comes to sales enablement materials and assets, so those listed are to guide not to complete. As you learn more about your GTM strategy's effectiveness, you'll gain insight into where the tweaks need to be made. Then set the experiments, choose your winners and move onto the next optimization opportunity.

As with any good strategy, especially aligned strategies, you can clearly see that elements and assets like landing pages are cross functional and so they may repeat. However, if you run back through the exercises you undertake during ARISE, there's overlap there too. Repetitiveness in the right areas is useful, but don't get too caught up in approaching these things from the individual lists; rather, comprehensively apply the suggestions in one area—like landing pages—to share your findings with your colleagues.

Arise GTM Strategy for Continuous Improvement

I'm going to close the book out with a recap on the ARISE Go-To-Market Methodology® and how you apply that for continuous improvement loops before delivering my final conclusion of the future of go to market strategy. Let's break this down stage by stage.

Assess

- Content Review
- Website Performance Analysis
- HubSpot/CRM Portal Audit
- Tech Stack Audit
- Persona Review
- Team Skills Assessment
- Product/Service Audit
- Reporting Performance Audit (sales, marketing, success, finance)

Research

- Competitive Analysis
- Customer Feedback
- Win/Loss
- Market Sizing
- Jobs to be done
- Third-party/Industry Resources

Ideate

- Positioning
- Messaging
- Value Proposition
- Storytelling
- Service Design

Strategise

- Goal and Objectives
- Content Planning
- Personas and Segments
- Keyword Strategy
- Website Requirements
- Asset Requirements
- Paid Marketing Strategy
- Reporting
- HubSpot Requirements
- Tech Stack
- Sales Enablement
- Customer Onboarding

Execute

- Pipeline Segmentation
- Sales, Marketing, and Success Playbooks
- Content Updates
- Website
- HubSpot Workflows and Sequences
- Paid Ads
- KPIs
- Quarterly Reviews

Conclusion

The Future of Go-to-Market Strategy

THIS IS IT. The final chapter; you've made it to the start line and I want to thank you for your perseverance. ARISE will continue to develop and I hope you take this approach and make it your own. I say that it's the start line because some folks read books like this and simply dive in and others get to the end and then start their journey. Whatever you do, however you approach this, I do hope to see how you use this; please do share with me via the website.

Now, let's look at emerging trends in go-to-market and how to stay ahead in a competitive market.

When I think of the emerging trends, right now it's one big one and that is AI. It's not only impacting every aspect of the workplace, it's impacting our lives. From automating everyday mundane tasks to comprehensively working toward solving some of the world's hardest problems and medical situations, AI isn't emerging; it emerged and all it will do is keep evolving.

AI in Marketing

For marketers, AI has already made a big impact; nearly every new email in your inbox is Martech with AI included and it's been added to everything we already use to boot. From graphic design to website builders, competitive research to data analysis, AI is in everything marketers do; our job is to establish where it's most effective for our individual business and double down.

AI in Sales

Sales teams have been using AI for longer than marketing. Tools like Gong, Ebsta, and Salesforce have all had AI behind the scenes analyzing things, so while it may not have directly been used, it was already enabled. Now sales reps and leaders have AI that automates outbound, inbound, calling, CRM administration, prospecting, and more. Their whole job is now AI enabled, which should help build strong results. Has anyone come out and yelled that AI is king in sales and defined the killer strategy that gave another 20% in revenue? No, not yet. But someone will figure it out soon enough. AI insights in real-time are what's needed, but AI triggered outcomes in real-time is where it should be at.

AI in Customer Services

Unfortunately, companies are seeing AI as another way to cut operational costs at the expense of the customer experience. Why on earth you would move to a wholly AI Agent support system is beyond me. They're good, great on occasion, but they are not the best solution every time. Even with HubSpot, the bots provide good service but they have the balance with a bot-first approach, supported by humans if need be. That is the ideal hybrid model for when a frustration can be prevented from becoming a churn event. Be mindful that cost saving looks good on the books, but often wears badly on the customer.

AI in Product

This is where the game changes. I don't think anyone is safe anymore, well any new tech that is. Incumbents like HubSpot have the financial muscle and power with AI to reproduce micro platform services within the CRM at scale and speed. I think we are about to see a new spree of M&A activity in the marketplace and a consolidation of tools rather than a huge expansion—all AI enabled by the way.

AI with People

I think AI will be a challenge for Gen Z. Already under fire for their lack of social skills in the office environment and often unrealistic demands for pay raises and promotions in unrealistic timeframes, the future of AI looks like a safe space for those with tenure and extended business acumen. As this book outlines I am a big believer in first-party data or knowledge being supported or enhanced with AI capabilities. Without committing to dedicating more time to professional development, I feel this could be a huge stumbling block for a whole generation.

If these simple forecasts are anything to go by, I feel you stay ahead by staying alert to the ecosystem. CMOs get off of your highchairs and back on the grass; you should engage with AI more as the appetite for AI enabled business leaders will almost certainly scale as fast as the landscape. And truly it's not just for CMOs but the wider C-Suite in all roles and middle management. Education is the future of growth and talent that is AI savvy and competent. But let me say this, for all that AI is worth, I also believe that tenure and experience are where it's at now. As I have said on more occasions than one in this book, first-party data and AI. Now, it's first-party knowledge and AI to have your own competitive advantage.

If you enjoyed what you've read in *Go-To-Market Uncovered*, we also developed a course you can take to certify in ARISE, and it's CPD accredited so you can use your corporate training budget if need be. Visit the website in the Appendix to access all supporting materials and offers.

Appendix

ALL MATERIALS REFERENCED in this book are available at www.arisegtm .com/book-registration where readers can register to get access to a private portal and bonus materials.

For those readers who would like to take our CPD accredited course on ARISE GTM please register at the site at https://arisegtm .com/go-to-market-strategy-mini-mba where you can access the course. For those who register for the portal, we will send you a personalized discount code for the course.

For those readers who would like to discuss consulting or coaching services, please contact me via the website at https://arisegtm.com/ contact-arise-gtm and I'll get back to you as soon as possible.

For those interested in becoming an ARISE certified GTM coach, register your interest at https://arisegtm.com/gtm-coaching-program.

For any press or speaker inquiries, please contact pr@arisegtm.com.

Glossary of Technologies

Mixpanel Mixpanel enhances go-to-market strategies by providing in-depth analytics of user interactions, enabling businesses to optimize their marketing efforts and measure the effectiveness of their sales processes. This data-driven insight supports product-led growth and improves customer acquisition and retention tactics.

Fathom Fathom enhances virtual meeting outcomes through its AI notetaking capabilities, streamlining communication and data retention, which informs product, marketing, and team strategies effectively.

Fireflies Fireflies.ai streamlines go-to-market strategies by automating meeting transcription and summarizing key insights, allowing teams to focus on discussions and collaboration rather than note-taking. This promotes timely follow-ups and enhances organizational communication, critical for effective market engagement.

Chat GPT ChatGPT enhances go-to-market strategies by providing valuable insights through market analysis and customer research, allowing businesses to effectively target their audiences and improve engagement through tailored content creation.

Claude Claude AI enhances go-to-market strategies by generating high-quality content, analyzing market trends, and personalizing marketing messages. This helps marketers automate tasks and focus on strategic initiatives, improving engagement and targeting precision.

Perplexity.ai   Perplexity.ai enhances go-to-market strategies by providing advanced search intelligence that helps teams identify market trends, customer preferences, and sales patterns. It facilitates streamlined product research and supports data-driven decision-making, ultimately driving revenue growth.

WordPress   WordPress is a powerful content management system that supports effective digital marketing strategies by enabling easy content creation, SEO optimization, and seamless integration with various marketing tools, ensuring that businesses can efficiently engage their target audiences.

Screaming Frog   Screaming Frog is a powerful SEO tool that helps websites improve their search engine visibility by auditing for common technical SEO issues. It identifies areas for improvement such as broken links, duplicate content, and metadata discrepancies, thus providing actionable insights that support effective go-to-market strategies for businesses aiming to enhance their online presence and drive traffic.

SEMRush   SEMrush is a comprehensive digital marketing platform that enhances online visibility and equips businesses with tools for SEO, PPC, and content marketing. It enables effective go-to-market strategies by providing insights into market opportunities and competitive analysis, which helps refine targeted messaging and positioning.

GT Metrix   GT Metrix helps businesses optimize their website performance, providing insights essential for enhancing user engagement and conversion rates, thus supporting effective go-to-market strategies.

Pingdom   Pingdom provides real-time insights into website performance and uptime, enabling businesses to address issues promptly and enhance the user experience. This is vital for retaining customers and optimizing marketing strategies.

Google Lighthouse   Google Lighthouse enhances go-to-market strategies by providing essential performance, accessibility, and SEO audits, helping businesses optimize their websites for better user experience and higher conversion rates.

AHREFS Ahrefs leverages a product-led content marketing strategy that creates valuable content aligned with their SEO tool, focusing on keyword research to meet user intent and build audience engagement, which can significantly enhance a company's market positioning.

PortallQ HubSpot auditing tool for CRM optimization, ensuring effective use of HubSpot for marketing, sales, and customer support.

Zapier Zapier enhances go-to-market strategies by automating workflows and integrating over 7,000 applications, allowing businesses to reduce manual tasks, improve efficiency, and focus on delivering impactful marketing campaigns.

Make Make serves as a technology platform that facilitates seamless user interactions and helps businesses create and implement effective go-to-market strategies by enabling precise targeting, optimizing marketing efforts, and enhancing overall customer engagement.

Respondent.io Respondent.io is a market research platform that connects researchers with high-quality participants, enabling efficient scheduling and feedback collection for user research. This platform streamlines the research process by simplifying participant recruitment and enhancing the quality of insights gained from studies.

Wynter Wynter is a B2B market research platform that provides rapid insights and feedback from target audiences, helping businesses refine their messaging and align their go-to-market strategies. This capability allows businesses to achieve better product-market fit and make informed marketing decisions based on actual customer perspectives.

G2 G2 empowers go-to-market strategies by leveraging real-time buyer intent data, allowing vendors to identify who is currently researching their products. This insight enables companies to engage potential buyers effectively and optimize their marketing efforts, enhancing demand and driving sales.

Capterra Capterra enhances go-to-market strategies by providing a platform for user reviews and software comparisons, enabling businesses to make informed software choices while allowing vendors to increase their product visibility through targeted advertising.

Trustpilot Trustpilot enhances go-to-market strategies by leveraging customer reviews to build brand trust and improve engagement. It allows businesses to integrate reviews in marketing communications, significantly influencing consumer purchase decisions and driving conversion rates.

Spendbase   Spendbase is an SaaS management platform that offers visibility into software subscriptions, optimizes costs, and manages renewals, enabling organizations to negotiate better vendor terms and maximize savings while maintaining control over software expenses.

Cledara   Cledara enables businesses to manage and optimize their software subscriptions efficiently, providing centralized visibility and control, thereby facilitating better alignment with market demands in their go-to-market strategies.

Reddit   Reddit's marketing potential lies in its ability to connect brands with highly engaged audiences in targeted communities (subreddits), allowing for precise targeting and organic reach that can facilitate brand engagement and virality.

Rollworks   RollWorks enables businesses to maximize revenue by focusing their marketing efforts on high-value accounts through account-based marketing (ABM). The platform uses intent data to identify potential customers and ensures marketing and sales alignment, ultimately increasing efficiency in go-to-market strategies.

Typeform   Typeform provides go-to-market teams with a platform to streamline customer acquisition and create engaging experiences that enhance lead conversion. Its capabilities allow businesses to capture zero-party data and personalize customer interactions, crucial for increasing engagement and driving revenue growth.

Similarweb   Similarweb empowers businesses to craft data-driven go-to-market strategies by offering detailed insights into market research, competitive analysis, and audience engagement. It enables users to identify their target market, monitor competitors, and optimize digital marketing strategies based on real-time data and performance benchmarks.

Clay   Clay acts as a versatile platform for data enrichment and outreach automation, allowing go-to-market teams to streamline lead generation, automate workflows, and improve lead conversion processes. By integrating AI, Clay enhances sales outreach with personalized messaging and efficient data analysis.

6Sense   6Sense enables sales and marketing teams to identify buyer intent and automate engagement, facilitating targeted campaigns that drive efficient revenue growth. Its predictive analytics help pinpoint high-potential accounts and support unified sales and marketing efforts.

Demandbase   Demandbase is an account-based go-to-market platform that helps B2B companies identify, engage, and convert their target accounts efficiently. By aligning marketing and sales efforts with data-driven insights, it automates marketing strategies to enhance revenue growth and supports dynamic buyer journeys.

Terminus ABM   Terminus ABM supports B2B go-to-market strategies by enabling teams to engage high-value accounts with personalized, data-driven marketing efforts that align marketing and sales, thus optimizing revenue generation.

N.Rich   N.Rich is a powerful account-based go-to-market (GTM) platform that enhances marketing strategies through scalable ABM advertising and real-time opportunity attribution, allowing businesses to effectively engage with high-potential accounts using intent data to drive revenue.

Cascadeapp   Cascadeapp is a strategy execution platform that helps organizations see faster results from their strategies and align objectives across multiple teams. It allows businesses to create cohesive go-to-market strategies that ensure efficient tracking and adaptation to market changes.

Leadfeeder   Leadfeeder is a B2B lead generation tool that provides sales and marketing teams with insights about which companies visit their website, enabling these teams to generate high-quality leads and optimize outreach efforts. By tracking anonymous website visitors and revealing their behavior, Leadfeeder allows businesses to connect proactively with potential customers who have already shown interest, thus effectively enhancing lead generation and conversion strategies.

Leadinfo   Leadinfo optimizes lead generation by providing real-time insights into website visitor behavior, enabling companies to identify high-quality leads and tailor their marketing strategies effectively. This enhances customer acquisition and streamlines the sales process.

Hotjar   Hotjar's platform provides insights into user behavior through video based evidence, enabling businesses to optimize their digital experiences effectively.

Apollo   Apollo enhances go-to-market strategies by providing a unified sales intelligence platform that integrates data intelligence with engagement tools and AI-driven assistance, enabling sales teams to efficiently identify and engage leads to drive revenue.

Breeze.ai Breeze.ai is an AI-powered suite integrated into HubSpot, designed to automate processes in marketing, sales, and service, thereby boosting productivity, enabling insightful content generation, and streamlining workflows for go-to-market teams.

Gong Gong enhances go-to-market strategies by providing revenue intelligence through the analysis of sales interactions, enabling teams to gain actionable insights, optimize outreach, and personalize training, therefore driving revenue growth effectively.

Bombora Bombora's platform provides businesses with intent data that identifies prospects ready to buy, allowing for targeted sales and marketing strategies. This helps optimize go-to-market efforts by focusing on accounts actively researching relevant topics and engaging them effectively before competitors do.

Pendo Pendo enhances product-led growth strategies by providing actionable insights into user behavior, improving onboarding processes and user engagement. Its integrations allow go-to-market teams to access behavioral data, enabling personalized experiences that strengthen customer relationships and drive conversion rates.

Chameleon Chameleon enhances go-to-market strategies by improving user onboarding and product activation through personalized in-app experiences, which drive higher user engagement and retention rates.

Partnerhub Facilitates partnerships between SaaS companies and digital agencies, expanding reach and distribution channels for go-to-market efforts.

PartnerStack Provides access to a large network of B2B partners and tools for managing partner relationships, enhancing distribution and sales channels.

Reveal Helps leverage partner ecosystems for revenue growth by identifying mutual customers and prospects, improving targeting and deal acceleration.

Crossbeam Enables ecosystem-led growth by identifying mutual accounts between partners, helping build stronger pipelines and expand market reach.

Acknowledgments

I'D LIKE TO thank everyone who contributed to my early career. From Martin Fenton, my first manager at JP Morgan, who gave me a shot as a non-graduate when grads were all they did, to Corrado Mortali at Commerzbank, who allowed me to kickstart my entrepreneurial journey while I was contracted to his department. Also, those managers who provided more challenging environments; those challenges made me understand the value of choosing to do things my own way and to question things I disagreed with.

In all the teams I've managed and been part of, I learned something from everyone, including my family and friends, who challenged me in ways you couldn't understand and are too varied to list. I appreciate each and every one of you.

I also want to thank social media. The imposter syndrome I had to overcome as I created the ARISE go-to-market methodology was hard. However, the variety of labels for "Go-to-Market" ensured that a clarified explanation was needed and would help me develop the proper terminology. Well, maybe that's my ambition.

Thank you to everyone who called me a trier, an ideas man, or labeled my early business "a project." I harnessed that energy to drive forward, as I always will. Hopefully, if any of you read this, you can see where big ideas go. I hope you get something out of this that helps your business journey as a business owner or a working professional.

Finally, and almost most importantly, thanks to my team at Wiley for the support, energy, and drive to complete the book turnaround and the advice you offered. I look forward to seeing how we develop.

About the Author

Paul Sullivan has more than 18 years of experience working with companies to develop business strategies. He began his career in investment banking, finding himself semi-automating his first role at JP Morgan and further involved in automation projects at Credit Suisse First Boston, Morgan Stanley, and UBS.

This natural aptitude for understanding business processes and how technology should facilitate them drove his exit from finance in 2008. However, the first stop was not into tech; it was into publishing and launching a lifestyle magazine called *Distinct*. Realizing that advertising revenue from lifestyle businesses wasn't a growth option, he pivoted into e-commerce, working with companies like Sky, Adidas, and others, before a client buy-out saw him become a de facto CTO for gaming app MyVote after four years.

After MyVote, he spent three years as a business consultant and held advisory and mentorship roles. He works at his tech consultancy, ARISE GTM (formerly Digital BIAS), a HubSpot agency partner launched in 2017 and his GTM Strategy startup, Leevr.

In 2024, he launched Digital Reform, a company that works with prison inmates to upskill them to the latest standards across marketing, sales, and customer success and a more substantial opportunity to integrate back into society.

Paul has been a consistent student throughout his career, spending equal time on personal and professional development. In 2021, he became a father to a daughter he adores. He balances his work and personal life, indulging in his passion for supporting his childhood club, Tottenham Hotspur, as a season ticket holder.

Index